Security in the Bubble

Globalization and Community

Susan E. Clarke, *Series Editor*
Dennis R. Judd, *Founding Editor*

VOLUME 24
Security in the Bubble: Navigating Crime in Urban South Africa
CHRISTINE HENTSCHEL

VOLUME 23
*The Durable Slum: Dharavi and the Right to Stay Put in
Globalizing Mumbai*
LIZA WEINSTEIN

VOLUME 22
*The Fragmented Politics of Urban Preservation: Beijing, Chicago,
and Paris*
YUE ZHANG

VOLUME 21
Turkish Berlin: Integration Policy and Urban Space
ANNIKA MARLEN HINZE

VOLUME 20
*Struggling Giants: City-Region Governance in London, New York,
Paris, and Tokyo*
PAUL KANTOR, CHRISTIAN LEFÈVRE, ASATO SAITO,
H.V. SAVITCH, AND ANDY THORNLEY

VOLUME 19
*Does Local Government Matter? How Urban Policies Shape Civic
Engagement*
ELAINE B. SHARP

VOLUME 18
Justice and the American Metropolis
CLARISSA RILE HAYWARD AND TODD SWANSTROM, EDITORS

(*continued on page 167*)

Security in the Bubble

Navigating Crime in Urban South Africa

Christine Hentschel

Globalization and Community, Volume 24

UNIVERSITY OF MINNESOTA PRESS
MINNEAPOLIS · LONDON

Portions of chapter 3 appeared previously in Christine Hentschel and Julie Berg, "Policing South African Cities: Plural and Spatial Perspectives," in *Police, Policing, Policy, and the City in Europe*, ed. Marc Cools, Sofie de Kimpe, Arne Dormaels, Marleen Easton, Els Enhus, Paul Ponsaers, Gudrun Vande Walle, and Antoinette Verhage, 147–73 (The Hague: Eleven International Publishing, 2010); in Christine Hentschel, "Outcharming Crime in (D)urban Space," *Social Dynamics* 37, no. 1 (2011): 148–64, http://www.tandf online.com; in Christine Hentschel, "Outcharming Crime in (D)urban Space," in *Rogue Urbanism: Emergent African Cities*, ed. Edgar Pieterse and AbdouMaliq Simone, 339–51 (Auckland Park: Jacana Media and African Centre for Cities, 2013); and in Christine Hentschel, "City Ghosts: The Haunted Struggles for Downtown Durban and Berlin Neukölln," in *Locating Right to the City in the Global South*, ed. Tony Samara, Shenjing He, and Guo Chen, 195–217 (New York: Routledge Studies in Human Geography, 2013), http://www.tandfonline.com.

Portions of chapter 4 appeared previously in Christine Hentschel, "'We Are Durban!' Städtische Angst und Sicherheit im Instant Space," in *Mega-event und Stadtentwicklung im globalen Süden: Die Fußballweltmeisterschaft 2010 und ihre Impulse für Südafrika*, ed. Christoph Haferburg and Malte Steinbrink, 117–39 (Frankfurt am Main: Brandes and Apsel, 2010); copyright Brandes & Apsel Verlag, Frankfurt.

Published by the University of Minnesota Press
111 Third Avenue South, Suite 290
Minneapolis, MN 55401-2520
http://www.upress.umn.edu

Library of Congress Cataloging-in-Publication Data

Hentschel, Christine, author.
Security in the bubble: navigating crime in urban South Africa / Christine Hentschel.
    ISBN 978-0-8166-9431-0 (hc)
    ISBN 978-0-8166-9432-7 (pb)
1. Crime—Political aspects—South Africa. 2. Crime prevention—South Africa.
3. South Africa—Politics and government—1994- . 4. South Africa—Social conditions—1994- . 5. Urban policy—South Africa. 6. City and town life—South Africa. I. Title. II. Series: Globalization and community; v. 24.
    HV7150.5.H45 2015
    364.0420968—dc23

                                                                    2014046649

Printed in the United States of America on acid-free paper

The University of Minnesota is an equal-opportunity educator and employer.

21 20 19 18 17 16 15   10 9 8 7 6 5 4 3 2 1

Contents

Acknowledgments   vii

Introduction   *Spatial Governance from Death to Life*   1

1. The Politics of Crime and Space in South Africa   15

2. Seeing Like a City   *Conceptual Devices*   41

3. Handsome Space   *Governing through Flirting*   57

4. Instant Space   *Governing through Fleeing*   89

Conclusion   *Making Love to the City*   117

Notes   125

Index   163

Acknowledgments

This book owes a great debt to the inspiration, camaraderie, and support of many people and institutions. I am grateful for the generous funding by the Hamburger Institute for Social Research and the Studienstiftung des deutschen Volkes; both enabled me to conduct extended research journeys in Durban and to write my doctoral thesis without financial worries. The ICI Berlin, the Legal Cultures Program of the Institute for Advanced Study in Berlin, and the Einstein Foundation supported me with postdoctoral stipends that allowed me to transform my dissertation into this book while working from Berlin.

I am grateful to those who became mentors over the years. Ulf Engel from the University of Leipzig was the first to encourage me to embark on this research, and he gently helped me walk through the entire process. Clifford Shearing offered invaluable intellectual support and involved me in inspiring conversations during long walks in the Cape area. Edgar Pieterse helped me discover the world of writing African cities and generously invited me to be part of the African Urbanism Initiative. The discovery of the Johannesburg Workshop in Theory and Criticism (JWTC) was eye opening, and I would like to thank Achille Mbembe, Kelly Gillespie, Julia Hornberger, and Leigh-Ann Naidoo for creating such a powerful space for "thinking from the South." The JWTC made me again aware of the special place that South Africa is and of the joy and care one should take in trying to write from and about it. John and Jean Comaroff strongly influenced me, and our brief conversations were some of the richest intellectual encounters I've had over those years. I am also deeply grateful to Mariana Valverde for the inspiration I could find in her work from the get-go, and for becoming a great interlocutor at the very end, when the manuscript was done. Susanne Krasmann gave me excellent advice at key moments of my writing and seemed to understand from the beginning what I was trying to do.

As I was growing into the field of urban studies, it was Talja Blokland who generously offered me a new home in Urban Sociology at Humboldt University, Berlin, pushed me to commit to southern urbanism, and made me want to study more closely the concrete social realities beyond the distant angle of "governance." Suzi Hall became a great colleague at a distance, and her own approach to urban ethnography reminded me why it is nice to care about good work. Maliq Simone arrived out of nowhere, it seemed, as one of the nicest surprises of my intellectual life.

I am grateful to many professionals and activists in the practical field of security in Durban. While all of them were generous with their time and knowledge, some of them went out of their way in helping me with orientation, connections, and pieces of information, and offering their analyses of what's going right and wrong in the city. Among the many to whom I am grateful are Abdull Domingo, Kay Butler, Chris Overall, Val Melis, Hoosen Moolla, and Richard Dobson.

A number of friends, co-conspirators, and members of working groups generously read and commented on early versions of my chapters. They include Brigitte Bargetz, Nadine Blumer, Heather Cameron, Anne Dölemeyer, Monika Eigmüller, Anja Feth, Gunilla Fincke, Angela Flury, Magdalena Freudenschuss, Jana Hönke, Sonja John, Uta Liebeskind, and Katrin Pahl, as well as the Berlin NYLON group. Looking at the dozens of drafts or papers with their handwritten comments in the margins and between the lines makes me grateful for the seriousness and sense of detail with which they engaged my early texts and for their constant encouragement. Other colleagues, spread all over the world, helped shape my ideas—Hillary Angelo, Jane Bennett, Colin McFarlane, Monique Marks, Bradley Rink, Jenny Robinson, Karen Rodriguez, and Tony Samara.

I had amazing, patient, meticulous, and creative English editors, to whom I extend my deep gratitude: Luita Spangler and Adam Armstrong for the very early drafts, and Ray Daniels, Angela Flury, and Sue Breckenridge for the late and final drafts. All of them held my hand when I was trying to walk the fine line between linguistic inventiveness and the clumsiness of an alien to the English language, and as often, the linguistic inaccuracies that they pointed me to turned out to emerge from my uncertainty in the argument itself. I also owe a lot of thanks to Conny van Heemstra for doing the long and often boring work of transcribing dozens of interviews, and to Ulrike Bialas for her brilliant research assistance when it came to the final strokes of the book manuscript.

At the University of Minnesota Press I want to thank my editor Pieter Martin and his assistant Kristian Tvedten, and the series editor Susan Clarke for their enthusiasm and their commitment to my project, as well as Martin Murray for reviewing and commenting so carefully on the complete manuscript.

Finally, I want to thank Rita Bakacs and Gunilla Fincke for being such outstanding, smart, and funny friends over those years, and Marie Klingelhöfer, who, by teaching me the pleasures of tango dancing, saved me from submerging during those times when writing was tough—right up to today. Thanks also to Kelly Gillespie and Leigh-Ann Naidoo, Dave Southwood, and John Cartwright without whose hospitality my research journeys would only have been half as much fun. My parents, sister, brother, their kids, and my late grandmother all trusted that the long process of researching and writing would lead somewhere; my thanks go to their optimism and unconditional love.

Spatial Governance from Death to Life

Dystopian Urbanism and the Bubble

The contemporary urban has been painted as a bleak, dystopian landscape of growing segregation and social apartheid.[1] From Detroit to Johannesburg, from Sao Paulo to Los Angeles, privilege is preserved through more exclusionary forms and coercive means than ever before, marking a "return of repression."[2] At the core of such aggressive urban spatialities is urban fear. Craving security, the middle classes withdraw behind "fortified enclaves," surrounded by the "dead space of blighted zones with decaying infrastructures, [and] inadequate service delivery."[3] Yet, beyond the brutal mechanisms of postmodern urbanism, other spatial forms are surfacing in people's daily strivings for security in the city. This book sets out to discover and conceptualize the details that the dystopic perspectives fail to perceive. While most critical urban and criminological scholarship engages with the secluded, barbed, and exclusionary forms of urban security, this book examines newly emerging aesthetic, affective, and inclusionary spatialities of security governance and points to the consequences for rethinking fragmentation, citizenship, and urban life.

Urban South Africa is an especially pertinent site for such an endeavor. While apartheid was spatial governance at its most brutal, postapartheid urban governance has rearticulated the politics of urban space. Critics have dismissed this spatial reinvention as nothing more than the addition of a layer of class segregation onto apartheid's racial morphology, but there is more to say on the contemporary self-reinvention of postapartheid urban spaces.[4] Twenty years after apartheid, spatial politics are no longer reducible to the after-pains of racial apartheid nor to a new class segregation. Governing (through) space has become a sophisticated polyphonic undertaking in which affective and communicative spatial strategies meld with more entrenched and rigid forms of spatial governance. Those complex spatiopolitical formations need a language more nuanced than "fortress cities," "enclaves," "class segregation," and "repressive governance."

I suggest the imaginary of the "bubble" to grasp the contemporary landscape of governance in the postapartheid city. Bubbles of governance are temporal spaces of different size, purpose, and modes of operation.[5] They can be porous or impermeable, place bound or mobile. They linger on entrenched architectures of segregation or assemble themselves into an entirely different landscape of fragmentation. Bubbles have different affective states and life spans. They are looked after by various actors and have distinct demographic profiles and crime rates. They can be private or public spaces, formally or more informally governed. Regardless of their many possible variations, all bubbles share a common definition: they are articulated urban chronotopes (space-times) of attention and regulation in the name of security.[6] As such, a bubble is a space longing for safety. How this longing is materialized in regimes of governance is the interest of this book.

Throughout this book, I will trace the contours of two emerging spatialized regimes of governing security in contemporary Durban, which I term *handsome space* and *instant space*. Handsome space reconstructs city makers' and security experts' taste for aesthetic and affective communication as a means of making their places safe.[7] Handsome space is about the making of safe bubbles (i.e., bars, parks, city improvement districts, or informal parking lots) through the power of flirtation. If flirting is a "pregnancy of possibility," flirting with and through space is meant here as the promise of (spatially and temporally limited) moments of security.[8] This flirting is itself spatial as it draws on spatial actants from music to wall decoration to convey a sense of security.

Instant space, on the other hand, follows the personal crime-related "navigation" systems of urban residents when they circulate through the city. While handsome space embraces the powers of flirting (in place-bound bubbles), instant space operates through the powers of fleeing (through mobile bubbles). Here, communicative, information-optimizing practices of self-help are intended to facilitate safe journeys for conscious and connected residents as they move through their city. In both regimes, security is not conceived as a public good, but rather as a situational experience that continuously needs to be renewed and can only be achieved through particularistic strategies against the commons of the city.

Security in the Bubble is about the political dilemma that this disjointed landscape of bubbles creates. In this sense, the bubble, throughout the book, remains an uneasy space, a space of uncertainty and exaggerated expectations. The bubble takes on a life of its own: it grows, stretches, lures—and eventually bursts. In other words, we cannot trust the bubble, that is, the space creating an illusion of safety, but we can, and should, take the risk of theorizing security governance through it nonetheless.

SPATIAL LIVES AND SPATIAL DEATHS

"Apartheid was a time of deadness," Sarah Nuttall writes, and adds: "Not only did it portend death for many, it implied a deadness in life for others, confined to townships, smothered by poverty, condemned to material and psychic dispossession. A pall of death, of deadness, hung over Johannesburg."[9] In apartheid, urban space was both the target and means of division and exclusion for a state obsessed with keeping populations apart from one another. An elaborate architectural apparatus of partitions, control posts, and gates was designed to forcibly prevent any encounters or movement among people classified as racially different. The designation of different groups to particular places of residence, work, transit, leisure, and the homogenization of these urban spaces can all be read into the spatial death that Nuttall describes. Indeed, apartheid spatial politics were, in Achille Mbembe's phrasing, "necropolitics": the "subjugation of life to the power of death."[10]

The end of apartheid marked the beginning of a new life for South African cities. Nuttall remarks: "South Africa now is alive, even as we live with death, dispossession, and poverty. This is an important difference; one can feel it in the deep fabric of the city at present, in this time. . . . It has become a place alive with emotion, struggle, passion, anger as well as inertia and disappointment."[11] South African inner cities, no longer white versions of urban modernity, have now been reinterpreted, both in function and aesthetics, by an almost entirely new urban population formerly confined to townships and by migrants from other African countries. Provisional housing in run-down office blocks, informal markets, and half-legal bars mushroom side by side with new shopping malls, development districts, and infrastructural projects.[12] On the level of urban politics, ideals of urban renewal, regeneration, and integrated development have invigorated city life and politics.[13] The transformation of space itself seems to have become the litmus test for successful urban transformation: from spatial death to spatial life.

At the same time, on an international level, a celebration of city life has inspired urban politicians and scholars alike. Creative city consultant Charles Landry advises city makers to embrace and shape their cities as "sensory, emotional experiences, for good and for bad."[14] City-brander extraordinaire Richard Florida proposes in *Who's Your City?* that cities have their own character and, just like life partners, should be chosen with care and love.[15] Many of these international trends invoke a consumerist understanding of "cityness" in which cities are brought into competition with one another—not just through their good infrastructure and reliable functioning, but equally through their particular vibe and appeal.[16] These notions that cities have their own lives are more than metaphors; they invoke a spreading imaginary of cities that speak a language, have a character, and, most importantly, possess the ability to affect people's emotions and actions.[17] Urban theory is also infected: urban sociology has explored the "intrinsic logic of cities," urban planning has experimented with "sense-scapes," and psychoanalytical geography has put cities with their emotional struggles onto "a big couch."[18]

Inspired by such international trends in affective urbanism and marked by their own dramatic history of space, South African urban politics have spatialized the thinking about urban social problems. Any attempts to undo the injustices of the past, it seems, when listening to city makers, must be spatial, and they must be spatial in a particular way, notably by pulling space from the realm of necropolitics toward the productive and aesthetic.

This postapartheid spatial fascination meets a tradition in North American and British criminology of spatializing crime and solutions to it. "Defensible spaces," "broken windows," "environmental design," and "situational crime prevention" all address crime as a problem of spatial management.[19] In the "non-utopian optimism" of mainstream criminology of the last decades of the twentieth century,[20] crime is seen as a normal social fact that does not require any particular pathology, and that needs to be understood in "dispassionate terms."[21] While Foucault identified how, at the turn of the nineteenth century, the criminal subject had emerged as the main focus of governmental interest, the "new culture of control" puts the fascination with the criminal offender aside and moves to "the criminogenic situation."[22] Since (potential) criminals are considered as rational as the rest of us, and assumed to decide on a cost-benefit analysis whether it is worth committing a burglary, here and now, the concrete shape of that very here-and-now matters. In the toolkits of situational crime prevention this means ensuring that potential targets are "hardened," "natural surveillance" enabled, property identified, and rules of the place communicated.[23]

Critical criminologists and urban sociologists have questioned the assumptions of these "criminologies of place" as simplifying or exaggerating the agency of place.[24] They have critiqued the limited spatial horizon of those criminologies and their complicity in deepening social and spatial fragmentation in the city.[25] And they have pointed to their exclusionary impulses and the discriminatory effects they have on the poor.[26] Involved in most of these critiques is a frustration with what Jock Young has called the "cosmetic fallacy:" the failure to address the root causes of crime while being obsessed with its superficial treatments.[27]

South African crime fighting politics are without doubt guilty of this cosmetic fallacy. But perhaps things are even more complicated. The seriousness with which city makers attribute the spatiality of a building, a park, or a club as the *reason* for its (in)security suggests that "surface" and "underneath" have been somewhat whirled around. Perhaps the root causes of violent crime are not simply neglected (as critical criminologists assume) but radically redefined. Contemporary anticrime measures do not search for the root causes of violent crime in a history of dispossession and dramatic inequality, but relocate and address them right on the urban surface. If we take these spatial surface obsessions seriously (as we should), we need to acknowledge the degree to which dysfunctional, badly shaped, disorderly places are seen as the root causes of criminal activities, while good-looking spaces with good ambience, orderly surfaces, and good taste are expected to create an aura of safety. The surface is not just superficial. It is at the root of current rationalities of urban governance and needs to be analyzed as such.

POSTCOLONIALIZING URBAN RESEARCH

Security in the Bubble is also a contribution to postcolonializing urban research. Urban studies, Jennifer Robinson argues, has long been divided between "Western and Other cities," between "celebrations of 'modernity'" on the one hand, versus "promotion of urban development" on the other.[28] Theory has, for too long, been produced in the North, and still passes for theory *tout court*.[29] The South, on the other hand, is studied as a collection of interesting, yet anomalous, empirical cases, "reservoir[s] of raw fact," or "objects to be theorized"—but is never able to theorize back, as it were.[30] In such a division of the urban world, African cities were, and still are, looked upon—or down on—as "the intractable, the mute, the abject, or the other-worldly," the bad example of something else, "a counterfeit modernity."[31] With the bulk of the urban experience of the twenty-first century taking place outside the West, it is time to embrace the fact that "the majority of the world does [indeed] produce *theory*."[32] The proposition of postcolonializing urban studies, then, is both modest and far reaching: urban scholarship, no matter where, needs to become "more cosmopolitan in [its] sources of inspiration and learning." This means decentering the usual (geographical and epistemic) reference points and writing theory from many places.[33]

What do we see, then, when looking at a world of cities from Africa? Misery and dysfunction? Lawlessness and chaos? Or the "sinister, dystopian aspects of postmodern urbanism," as some have argued?[34] New archives of writing African cities into theory, Nuttall and Mbembe argue, need to overcome any simplifying apocalyptic framings, ethnographic exoticisms, and developmental paradigms.[35] As Appadurai and Breckenridge paraphrase Mbembe's and Nuttall's endeavors to write "the world" from Johannesburg: "We will not wait, [Mbembe and Nuttall] argue, and we cannot afford to wait, to defer the writing of Africa until the day . . . when the world shall declare that Africa has now officially been allowed the privilege of having an everyday, of having an urban life, of having lives worth studying and styles worth emulating. . . . [This is] the refusal to allow the harder places on this planet to be chained to the fables of breakdown, malfunction, disrepair, and degradation."[36] Sources for "writing 'Africa'" into theory are diverse. They include the aesthetic and functional workings of everyday cityness, the entanglements of "surface and underneath," the invisible, ghostly orders of cities, and psychoanalytic readings of the city.[37] As Edgar Pieterse argues, "African cityness" can "broaden our grasp of non-Western cities by starting with the assumption that all cities are equivalent as distinct but intertwined repositories of modernity; i.e. banal and ordinary, but also harbingers of the capacity for extraordinariness and novelty."[38]

Security in the Bubble is an attempt to look at new archives from African urbanism in a conversation with spatial and governmentality literature that emerged in the West. How, for example, are the various ingenious modes of survival thematized in ethnographic accounts entangled with the practices of self-government that Foucault-inspired scholars write about? How is the struggle to produce the sense of stability and permanence that Mbembe and Simone identify as central features of African urban life interwoven with the logics of instant gratification and speculation that drive our current system of late capitalism?

Writing the World from Durban

So, what, or *who* is Durban, and why does Durban matter for understanding life and politics in other places in the world? Let me begin with "who Durban is," according to those involved in forging its image. Affectionately known as "Durbs," the city is the number one holiday destination for South Africans. Durban is South Africa's "warmest place to be," as the 2010 World Cup advertisement campaign put it.[39] The beachfront along the city very much defines its image and makes for its sun-and-surf-appeal, yet there is more here than meets the eye. Durban author Elana Bregin depicts the city's "character" as follows:

> If one had to characterize Durban's beachfront as an archetype, it would be the whore with the heart. Over the years she's been pretty much pimped to exhaustion; she's seen it, been it, done it all. Her natural assets of waves, sand, and famously good weather have never been sufficiently valued for the true treasures they are, and much of the original charm has been bulldozed from her by overzealous makeovers and tourist hard sell. Her best beaches have been colonized by casinos and marine world mega ventures. . . . No matter how many facelifts they give her, no matter how

they try to remodel and remake her, sweep the resident street kids out of sight, infuse some JHB [Johannesburg] class or CT [Cape Town] pazazz [*sic*] into her Eliza Doolittle, Point Road persona, she remains good-naturedly what she is: slightly seedy, slightly suspect, yet still charming in a raddled, rundown, overpriced sort of way.[40]

Durban, with its exhaustion and facelifts, its big heart and its seediness, is a city that has also grown immensely during its transition to becoming a postcolony. It has almost 3.5 million inhabitants, with 63 percent categorized as Zulu, 20 percent as people of Indian descent, and 9 percent as white. At 31.3 percent, Durban's poverty rate is very high, although it has declined slowly but steadily since its 2004 peak. It is also an extremely unequal city, with a Gini Index of 0.61, almost as high as that of the world's least equal country.[41] Durban's unemployment rate, although down from 43 percent in 2001, at 30.2 percent was still immense in 2011.[42]

Crime in Durban is high. According to a survey conducted by the municipality, 17 percent of Durban's population was a victim of crime in 2010/11, with burglary, robbery, car theft, assault, and hijacking officially ranging among the most common ones.[43] Accounts of crime and violence pervade ordinary conversations, as do warnings. When darkness falls over Durban, a different time regime takes over the city. The middle classes try to get out of downtown Durban, and those left in the inner city, it seems, are either courageous, careless, clueless, or criminal. Durban novelist Imraan Coovadia warns that even driving requires special precautions: "people don't stop at red lights after seven in the evening for fear of being hijacked."[44] In Durban, "the world doesn't end in the abstract; it ends practically. The police stations and the courts don't function. There is not a road in Durban where a woman feels safe after dark. Durban, South Africa's Indian Metropolis, is always on the brink of ruin."[45] How, then, can we imagine the story of Durban entangled with the various urban elsewheres? And in what sense does the unique case of a postapartheid city by South Africa's Indian Ocean with warm sun and appalling crime rates provide insights into trends in urban governance at large? The answer to these questions must first acknowledge what South Africa has come to mean to the world. During the apartheid decades, it was iconic for its brutal history of segregation and served as a "negative role model for urban planners in other parts of the world."[46] More recently, it has become infamous for its grave social inequalities and enormous crime rates, but it is also celebrated for its unprecedented transition to democracy. A second answer has it that the story of a South African city is crucial, because we are witnessing the "south africaniza- tion of the world."[47] Following this line of thought, in looking at Dur- ban, we are looking at the world at large, one that "is looking ever more 'postcolonial,'" as John and Jean Comaroff claim.[48] Africa, especially, has "come to anticipate the unfolding history of the global north," because in Africa, the "material, political, social, and moral effects of the rise of neoliberalism [are] most graphically evident."[49]

I take a more measured stance on "Why Durban?" Rather than seeing South Africa as uniquely extreme or identifying it as the world's future, I understand Durban as an "ordinary city," in which global trends "take place" and unfold in a particular way.[50] Or, put differently, Durban's legacy of urban segregation, the pervasive urban fear, and the weak stance of the state make it a particularly pertinent case for investigating trends in the governance of security and space that strongly resonate with developments in other places in this phase of late capitalism. I hereby seek to work on the potential for a truly comparative urbanism that is "at once more global and more situated in its claims" and engages all of these places as offering insight into urban life in the world at large.[51] I thus treat Durban as a prism in which international trends in spatial security governance meet and intertwine with local particu- larities that can hardly be found anywhere else. This, perhaps, is what the Comaroffs call the "awkward shifting scale" in which the phenom- ena we observe are "*both* global in its reach and localized in its protean manifestations."[52]

FROM GERMANY TO SOUTH AFRICA AND BACK

My own journey as a white woman from an East German village is itself part of this awkward shifting scale. Between September 2005, when I first arrived in Durban, and March 2009, I returned twice a year to carry out my empirical research. I was initially interested in investigating "underclass violence" and the role African intellectuals played in actively shaping such violence in the early twentieth century. But my journey in the archives became truncated as I became increasingly drawn into the contemporary politics of everyday violence in the city. The flood of warnings and advice that inundated me whenever I set out to walk around or take a bus, and the everydayness of brutal crime in people's stories and media coverage deeply disturbed me. I was puzzled by the overall inclination to solve social problems as complex as that of violent crime with a range of individualized small-scale solutions. The governmentality literature—the lenses through which I saw the world at the time—reflected on retreating tendencies of the state and the growing role of the individual, but it did not capture all the variations and depth that such trends appeared to take on in Durban. Likewise, the police did not "own" the fight against crime, nor were the police the chief managers in outsourcing this fight to a wider range of actors. Instead, when involved at all, they were only helpers or, some of the time, metaphorical figures whenever ordinary residents "played police." Security was a widespread concern that people from different professional fields and walks of life dealt with in their everyday, when they designed a park, decided on the music in their bar, and planned their journey through the city.

Any inquiry into the logics of security governance needed to reflect this complex "securisphere."[53] In more than seventy-five interviews, I talked to security professionals, including members of the police, private security guards, intelligence experts, and operators from municipal and private CCTV control rooms. I interviewed strategists and practitioners in the city's planning, architectural, health, and transport departments; representatives of Business Against Crime and Urban Improvement Precincts; hotel, bar and club owners; street traders; and informal car guards. I also asked radio reporters, community crime prevention groups, neighborhood watches, and active members of community police forums for their perspectives. Most of the interviews were recorded with a digital recorder, transcribed, and coded. Other conversations, especially with actors who operated at the fringes of legality—for example, informal bar owners, car guards, sex workers, or street traders—were not recorded.

I joined my interview partners at their shifts in various jobs and attended their strategy meetings and tried to understand the technological and legal tools they employ and the coalitions they seek to forge. I collected any internal communication that seemed relevant: plans and reports, correspondence and evaluations, drafts for prospective projects, professional guidelines, maps of various kinds, advertisement material and minutes of meetings. Alongside that, I compiled a wide set of public or semipublic messages in the forms of newspaper articles, radio reports, statistics, political speeches, newsletters, websites, crime blogs, or self-help guides. I imagine them as scraps of the city's "epistemic wallpaper" that both frame and reflect how urban residents problematize crime and act upon it.[54]

SECURITY, SUBJECTIVITY, AND "DOING SPACE"

My concern in *Security in the Bubble* is with the struggles of Durbanites to come to terms with life in the city as dangerous. Different theoretical traditions have analyzed the changing rationalities of government over the past decades. Governmentality scholars looking at European and North American contexts have established how the state pulls back and governs "at a distance," and citizens are "responsibilized" to care for an increasing realm of their own lives.[55] In African or Latin American contexts, where the Hobbesian dream was a reality of a different kind, the narrative on "outsourcing," "rolling back of the state," and "responsibilizing" had less of a grip. Because "the state" as a provider of public support systems and functioning infrastructures could not be taken for granted, residents in urban Africa had long been creating their own pathways to make things work. Urbanites had to improvise, muddle through, autoconstruct, and pirate, as we learn from anthropology and sociology.[56] Whether responsibilized or left alone, both accounts point the finger at an urban subjectivity "in charge."

Together responsibilization and survival complicate the meanings of citizenship. The city has become the substance and the strategy for many citizenship claims, and sociology has celebrated the rise of urban citizenship for its inclusive, direct, and democratic virtues.[57] But neither the "urban citizen" of political sociology, nor the "homo prudens" of critical governmentality, nor the "denizen" of security studies is adequately grasping urban subjectivities as they are organized around the pursuit of security.[58] The protagonists of *Security in the Bubble* are of a particular kind, and this has to do with the centrality of security itself in the changing rationalities of government. Over the last decades we have seen the "rise of the security paradigm as a framework for organizing contemporary social life."[59] We are governed "through security" and governed "through crime."[60] Risk has become a core technique of government, entangling citizenship and vulnerability in ever-new ways.[61]

If the concern for security is ubiquitous, "banal" even, how does it function as a governmental technique that works through space?[62] Over the course of this book I develop a device to look at the pursuit of security, namely that of *doing space*. Doing space, as I understand it, extends beyond the "grammar" of official planning acts; it involves the multiple "pedestrian speech acts" of the everyday.[63] Doing space, furthermore, is relational: If space is the "sum of interrelations," as Massey argues, doing space entails forging and reworking these interrelations, and it means making the social and material infrastructures that are "between us in the city."[64] Finally, doing space is performative. Space, Gillian Rose writes, is not only the product, but itself a strategy of power, "a matrix of play, dynamic and iterative, [and] its forms and shapes produced through the citational performance of self-other relations."[65] Doing space is thus about the complex ways in which space is enacted, opportunities are created, people sorted, and subjects made.

"Doing space," with its planned and everyday, relational and performative dimensions, is thus my analytical device for inquiring into the spatial side of security. Just like governing in the Foucauldian sense, doing space, as I see it, is not only about the sovereign, solid, and exclusionary manifestations of power, but also concerns the elusive, soft, inclusionary ones. Doing space in the pursuit of security, I will argue throughout the book, is affective, aesthetic, mobile, and communicative, and therefore raises a number of challenges for how we think about government, fragmentation, and citizenship.

Chapter Outlines

Chapter 1, "The Politics of Crime and Space in South Africa," builds a historical framework for understanding the politics of crime and space in urban South Africa and contextualizes themes crucial to the empirical analysis discussed later in the book, namely security deficits, segregation, and plural policing, as well as information and communication politics. It defines first the contours of the discourse on postapartheid crime and violence that pervades media, politics, and everyday life. Then it analyzes ways in which talking about, (dis)counting, and acting on crime in (white) cities and (black) townships were addressed in the past, and concomitantly provides an overview of state and non-state conducted security politics in posttransition South Africa. Turning to urban space, the second part of the chapter outlines the rationalities of governing apartheid spaces and subjects before examining postapartheid spatialities. The chapter thus begins to establish the core idea of the book: since space was central to apartheid urban ordering, it remains crucial in postapartheid strategies that seek to undo the injustices of the past. Governing through handsome and instant spaces can thus be read as endeavors to redraw a troubled spatial history.

Chapter 2, "Seeing Like a City," creates a methodology for defining security, governing, and the urban, and proposes an investigation into the processes and conditions through which these concepts become imagined and problematized in policing practices. It makes the case for breaking down what Valverde has called "seeing like a city"[66] into a variety of bubbles of security governance and suggests how to peer into these bubbles—notably through "low status" expert knowledge and "epistemic wallpaper."[67] Finally, I weave those thoughts together into my frame of regimes of spatial security governance.

Chapter 3, "Handsome Space," traces the rationale of security as a space-specific good that can best be achieved through the powers of aesthetics and affect. Drawing on security practices in various Durban spaces (a luxury district, an informal parking lot, an inner-city bar, a municipal bus project, and a busy traders' market), I chart how inner-city spaces of different scope, function, and use follow a remarkably similar preoccupation with their (orderly, appealing, tasteful) spatiality as the central means of ensuring their safety. Harder, more clearly exclusionary modes of spatial regulation are always entangled with these flirty techniques, but I want to tell the story the other way round, making room for the details of aesthetic and affective governance usually treated as the mere add-ons to broken-windows-style policing. In the final part of the chapter I reflect on the relationship between these handsome spaces as islands of (imagined) safety and (the rest of) the city and suggest ideas for rethinking urban fragmentation and social sorting. What does it mean for a social collectivity to tackle its drama of violence as hundreds of mini-problems, each residing in their own separate bubble, each being solved as its own "situation" against the commons of the city?

"Instant Space," chapter 4, shifts the perspective from tangible urban spaces to the everyday navigation and communication practices of urban subjects who make their way through the city, moving in and out of these supposed islands of safety that the makers of handsome space seek to create. Detailed, up-to-date, and ready-to-use knowledge about the spatial and temporal facts of crime in the city is key in this regime. Here, security is a situational, personal, yet networked practice of crime avoidance only achievable through a wide array of knowledge and com-munication strategies in the form of crime newsletters, SMS informa-tion systems, or self-help guides. According to this logic, insecurity and crime are accepted as social facts that while they cannot be overcome, can be measured, counted, visualized, communicated, and, if a person is lucky, individually avoided. While the regime of instant space has an ideal, "universal" citizen that I call *everyone,* there is also a large group of other subjects who cannot or do not want to fully embrace these strate-gies of instant crime prevention. Their selective involvement into the regime of instant space happens through a different set of registers: not through responsibility but through financial incitements and work obli-gations. The regime of instant space thus interpellates subjects of differ-ent "sorts," whose complex interwovenness with one another cannot be reduced to an in-group versus out-group kind of seclusion.

The concluding chapter formulates a number of prospects and chal-lenges to a scholarship committed to understanding and critiquing con-temporary forms of urban security governance and emerging fragmen-tations in our cities. If urban security is increasingly a micro-scaled, situational, and skillful practice of survival in the city, what remains of normative notions of security as a public and universal good?[68] If secu-rity becomes the very core of citizenship practices, what are the con-sequences for the concept of urban citizenship? If the world at large is looking ever more postcolonial, what insights can Durban's spatial life of security offer places like New York, London, or Berlin?

1

The Politics of Crime and Space in South Africa

In urban South Africa, a tremendous amount of violent crime is entangled with a dramatic history of space. One cannot be explained without the other. If South Africa is a "crime capital" and South Africans are "wallowing in [their] own blood," what is the history of governing (through) space that has created, and keeps creating, this "ruination"?[1] Visiting the ruins of apartheid history means not only looking at the past, or at the relics of a defunct regime as dead matter, but it also means tracing "the production of new exposures and enduring damage"—in urban landscapes, in politics, and in the common sense disturbed by these ruins.[2] This chapter will thus "place" the contemporary security regimes of handsome and instant space, which are developed later in this book, in a longue durée of spatiopolitical formations of segregation, insecurity, and survival.

In many ways, the character and language here are different from those that follow. This chapter discusses numbers and debates, while in later chapters, strategies and practices become more important. It relates crime to the history of apartheid and problematics of race, while later minor allusions will have to suffice to remind the reader of the context in which the regimes of handsome and instant space "take place."

In looking at national government programs, this chapter distinguishes between state policing and non-state policing, whereas thereafter, the formal and informal and the public and private converge along rationalities and practices. The "contemporary" from which this chapter departs is the postapartheid period at the end of the Mbeki and the beginning of the Zuma presidencies, between 2006 and 2009, pre–World Cup 2010. Numbers, debates, and policies discussed in this chapter very much belong to this phase. Only in some moments do I illuminate my point from the perspective of the most recent developments in South Africa.

THE POLITICS OF CRIME IN SOUTH AFRICA

South Africa postapartheid "continues to exist somewhere between war and peace," writes Tony Samara.[3] While the country did not fall into civil war in the years of transition, it fell into some other kind of "war with itself" and became one of the most crime-ridden nations.[4] This section reflects on the ways crime is talked about, counted, accounted for and policed, past and present. It links the problematics of crime to the waning legitimacy of the postapartheid state and reflects on the relationship between violent crime and race/racism. Finally, it sketches the plural nature of security governance in posttransition South Africa.

Crime Capital

The fear of crime pervades people's lives in South African cities, and many South Africans have adapted to a life in danger. In a side note to a story about Johannesburg (not a crime thriller!), literary theorist and writer Sarah Nuttall describes her nightly rituals of preparing herself for the possible:

> Each night . . . I would take my handbag with all my bank cards and licenses in it, my car keys, and my cell phone, and lay them on the dining room table . . . I would lay these things out, in a little row. They were a form of address. To the man who might make his way in. Take everything you want. The computers in the studies, the music system in the lounge. The car in the garage, the money in the bank. Just let us live.[5]

People's personal experiences and coping strategies are involved in a complex relationship with an impersonal and abstract sphere of crime statistics. Numbers, John and Jean Comaroff argue, are "quantifacts . . . statistical interpretations that make the world factual."[6] Not that South Africans need statistics to know that there is crime in their country, but these data form an infrastructure through which crime-talk flows through the public sphere. Through statistics the individual case becomes part of a shared urban nightmare that has profiles and patterns. According to the Comaroffs, statistics quantify, catalogue, measure, and translate human loss and suffering into numbers, but they also do the inverse: "Figures render large abstractions concretely meaningful to personal experience." They "reduce a mass of faceless incidents, . . . into objects of first-person affect: fascination, revulsion, pain."[7]

South African crime rates are high in international comparison. Crime statistics of the period studied in this book reveal that 18,148 people were murdered in South Africa between April 2008 and March 2009. Broken down to a daily rate, this amounts to an average of almost 50 people murdered per day—the lowest level since the peak of transition violence in 1994/95. In the same years, the "trio crimes"—house robbery, carjacking, and business robbery—have consistently risen and shaped the public imaginary about common threats.[8] To be sure, South Africa is not the only country with high crime rates. Comparative studies show sharp increases in crime and disorder as a worldwide by-product of states transitioning to democracy in the 1990s.[9] What makes South Africa "World Champion" is not its volume of crime, but its extraordinary *violence*.[10] A recent study reveals that almost one-third of all men admit to having raped once or many times.[11]

Yet, the current statistics might underestimate the actual scope of crime: Victimization reviews suggest that actual crime rates must be much higher than the figures indicate. In a 2006 survey Afrobarometer revealed that 32 percent of the respondents answered that they or someone in their family had something stolen from their house in the past year, and 17 percent said that they or someone in their family had been physically attacked in the past year. Compared to existing crime statistics, this would amount to far higher crime figures than reported by the South African Police Service (SAPS).[12]

Statistics are subject to a "paradox of dis/trust," John and Jean Comaroff reason.[13] They are at once a fetish and an object of suspicion. With the hunger for statistics comes a cynical conviction that the statistics could have gone "bad" by the time they left the police headquarters or the Ministry of Safety and Security. The stories about the sanitation of crime statistics and fraud from the station-level up to the national police nourish such a sense of distrust. The problem lies mainly in the fact that police performance is measured by the reduction of crime figures. Numerous interview partners in the Durban policing context revealed that, in order to meet the annual targets of a 7 to 10 percent reduction in various crime categories, fraud in recording and counting has become common practice, as has smartly distributing crimes to more harmless categories; for example, by moving "rape" to "indecent assault" or "car jacking" to "theft." A prosecutor for the National Prosecution Authority reported in an interview that such practices are indeed common within police stations and often derive from orders in the upper levels of police administration. To give the prosecutor's case scenario: "Basically we have for example . . . a syndicate that is hijacking trucks. Okay? So they hijack the driver, they take the truck, they sit here. The instruction is, if the police should recover the truck. . . . , the charge must be *theft of cell phone,* because *in the robbery* the driver's cell phone was taken."[14] In addition, police stations, seeking to bring crime (statistics) down, have avoided recording more crimes than "necessary" by only opening a case where a case number is mandatory (namely, when it involves death or insured property), or by discouraging people from filing a complaint in cases where it is not clearly required (i.e., in domestic violence situations).[15]

For example, in 2009 a KwaZulu-Natal constable caused public furor by exposing fraudulent activities in the collection of crime statistics in his station. According to the constable, his station commissioner instructed the detectives to proceed only with matters where "suspects are immediately available or easily ascertainable." Less promising dockets were to be stocked in a separate room, in order to be left out of the reporting system. When they started to pile up, many of them were burned. The strategy paid off: in August 2008 the station was commended as the top station in the province in regard to the percentage of reduction of crime statistics, with rewards consequently paid to each member of the police station. In a raid by the Independent Complaints Directorate, however, the remaining 170 unregistered dockets were found. The case was brought to court after the whistleblower was suspended and intimidated by his commissioner.[16]

Many have argued that such statistical sanitation practices are literally built into the system that pressures station commissioners to meet crime reduction targets, and this is certainly not a South African particularity. On the other hand, whenever figures go up, police are able to interpret this as a success resulting from more victims reporting their cases. Given these possibilities for modification, statistics remain a frustrating issue for the general public. People have good reason to be suspicious about statistics presented to them, and yet, they long for them and have made them an "ordinary language of being."[17] As John and Jean Comaroff write, "The crime statistic has taken on unprecedented sovereignty in this postcolony. It has not only become diagnostic of national health. It is also a discursive currency by means of which government speaks to its subjects, citizens speak among themselves, experts speak to everypersons, everyone speaks back to government, and the media mediate all the incessant talk, adding their own inventions, inflections, inflations."[18] The fascination with and the longing for crime figures goes far beyond a political discourse. In what I call *the regime of instant space* (chapter 4), I will show how the striving for numbers, profiles, and spatial data have entered the sphere of everyday practices of ordinary citizens' crime avoidance. Here, an ever-growing expertise is required of ordinary people to gather and share, to spatialize and trade knowledge about crime, and, by that, to stay safe.

The State at Stake

Whenever the government refuses to talk statistics, it meets outrage on the side of the opposition and civil society groups. Numbers are not only a measure of dis/order, a paradox of dis/trust, an index of the in/effectiveness of rule and of police or government performance. The free circulation of crime statistics has in itself become a symbol for and a vital ingredient of the new democratic public sphere and a means of self-reflection for the new South Africa—a form of communication that was suppressed by the apartheid state. Small wonder, then, the anger when government interrupts the flow of numbers, as happened, for example, when the (then) Minister of Safety and Security, Steve Tshwete, announced a moratorium on crime statistics in July 2000,[19] or when the newly appointed National Police Commissioner Bheki Cele expressed his support for a moratorium in August 2009, reasoning that criminals "could use the statistics."[20]

The hesitation to make crime statistics public is often interpreted as the government's refusal to acknowledge the actual scope of the problem. In an editorial in the *Sunday Times,* the authors accuse the African National Congress (ANC) government of closing their eyes in the face of the "country's out-of-control crime situation. . . . Like the proverbial ostrich, they refuse to accept that this country is under siege from criminals."[21] Such a refusal to acknowledge the crisis of crime touches the very core of democracy and endangers the major political achievements of the new South Africa, as the authors make explicit: "Can we as South Africans really proclaim that we are free people when we live in fear of the thousands of monsters that roam our streets? . . . Just like South Africa was freed from the yoke of apartheid, South Africa must be freed from the yoke of crime."[22]

The unfreedom of apartheid and the unfreedom of crime are often related to one another in such debates, implying that if the ANC managed to fight and defeat apartheid, it could and should also fight crime. But there are different ways of drawing a link between apartheid unfreedom and the postapartheid crisis of crime. In their piece "Crime and Politics in Our Time," Johannesburg-based scholars Deborah Posel, Julia Hornberger, and Achille Mbembe draw the link differently, relating current challenges of violent crime to the promise of the political transition in the South Africa of the 1990s. They argue that South Africa's transition from apartheid was, in part, an aspiration to overcome a history of "arbitrary, violent and corrupt state actions, which had gone hand-in-hand with a glamorization of popular violence, crime, and disregard for the law."[23] An even more widespread racial bloodbath than the one that took place was averted during the transition, they argue, but there was an implicit deal. The deal, to their thinking, was that of the democratic leviathan:

> At the heart of the negotiated settlement and the avoidance of racial violence was a tacit contract: The state, by way of constitution, would undertake to protect the lives of all South Africans equally, provided they renounced the recourse to violence. And reciprocally, that there should be a thoroughgoing popular respect for the law, as the appropriate instrument of justice—renouncing the idea that justice could be meted out privately, in institutions and practices beyond the control of the state.[24]

This consensus, they reason, is now put into question by the avalanche of crime, violence, and corruption. No less than the very project of state and democracy in South Africa is at stake: "As crime escalates and as criminals act with relative impunity, the ingredients of a democratic "social contract" corrode. If there is no safety or security in the idea and in the practice of law, if the state is unable to deal effectively with crime, and the propensity to lethal violence seeps across civil society, then what gives the democratic state its popular legitimacy?"[25] While the South African state still garners a great deal of its legitimacy from its defeat of apartheid, this might not be the case for much longer, Posel, Hornberger, and Mbembe prophesize. Increasingly, the legitimacy of the state "will be based in the present" and in the state's capacity to "deliver on the promise of democracy," especially to "protect the right to life."[26] In other words, "a state that cannot hold its citizens accountable for breaches of the law, cannot be entrusted with the project of democracy."[27] And, one might add, a state whose police shoot dozens of striking workers (as in the Marikana mine in August 2012) or tie a human being behind a police van and drag him to death (as happened to a Mozambican taxi driver in February 2013) cannot be entrusted with the project of safety or the defense of democracy. Violent crime in both apartheid and post-apartheid South Africa is intrinsically a crisis of the state.

"Apartheid Nostalgia"

The onslaught of numbers, pictures, and horror stories in the media, combined with the personal experience of precariousness, make some plunge into a sentiment that historian Gary Kynoch has coined "apartheid nostalgia."[28] In 2001–2 Kynoch interviewed residents of Soweto who had lived there during apartheid and who remembered the township of the apartheid era as being much safer, more orderly, and more predictable than today.[29] According to Kynoch, many respondents depicted the apartheid South African Police (SAP) as oppressive, but strict and capable of enforcing the law. The new postapartheid South African Police Service (SAPS), in contrast, is seen as more respectful and approachable, but corrupt and incapable of bringing down crime. Some interviewees even saw the pass laws, epitomes of apartheid oppression, as effective means of controlling people, not only politically, but also with regard to the possession of guns and knives, and criminal activities.[30]

Many expressed ambivalence concerning the idea that "even criminals have rights." In addition, people in the township community would take care of a criminal themselves and catch and beat him whenever there were no police.[31]

To be sure, these memories conflict with other historical accounts on township violence, systematic oppression, and deplorable life circumstances, including the sphere of personal security.[32] Kynoch himself is aware of the possible idealizations and distortions in the work of memory, yet he insists that these limitations do not invalidate Sowetans' perceptions of the past.[33] Put differently, even if these works of memory are highly selective, they still point to a number of crucial themes in thinking about crime—present and past.

Switching scenes, from the Johannesburg Township in 2002 to Durban's inner-city beachfront in 2007, a white hotel safety manager, responsible for security issues on the wider beachfront, expressed similar feelings of nostalgia when talking about the safety of "his" beach:

> D: Because, I don't know why, before 1994, it is not that I am a racist or from the old regime or whatever, I could walk on the beachfront. . . . It was safe, I could walk there, there was still a death penalty. You knew you gonna be killed as well. . . . People didn't sleep all over the whole world. I think, let's go back in national stats and look at mugging tourists in the country before 1994 and after the year 2000. Then, obviously, you see the difference. . . .
>
> CH: Who was at the beachfront before . . . the 1990s? Who had the right to the beach actually?
>
> D: You know, at one stage, you're right, I don't know if it was before 1994, only whites were allowed to the beachfront. I think that changed in 1994. Before '94, no, you're correct there; only whites had the right to go to the beach before 1994. . . . Which is "maybe wrong. I don't approve of that. Surely that was wrong. But if we go to the beach, we go to the beach to enjoy ourselves and to have a good life, or do we go there to get killed? That is what's changed. We've changed this thing about racism and everything, but now people get killed.[34]

The manager's suggestion, to look back at national crime statistics and then compare, points to a central problematic in the politics of crime:

the production and the representation of numbers, images, and strategies are part of particular truth regimes of crime. In fact, counting, measuring, and defining crime is a by-product of modern biopolitics and differs according to political systems, times, and places.[35] As Mana Slabbert states, "the process of creating crime statistics in any country is not unrelated to the political power structure within which definitions of crime and criminality are formulated."[36] Crime meant and means different things in the old and in the new South Africa. What activities were and are deemed criminal; who created and creates the rules for these definitions and in whose interest; who enforced and enforces these rules with what means: the answers to these questions have changed from apartheid to postapartheid. Thus, any reference to the past in debates about the present needs to take into account these changes and limitations.[37]

This means, first, considering the obvious: priorities for the South African state were different at different times. The apartheid government protected whites from the impact of crime with a system that sought to "isolate violence in black areas and prevent its spread to wealthy and white localities."[38] The general rationale was to police black populations and to protect whites. The majority of police resources were placed in city centers, sites of production, and white suburbs and towns. Violence in black areas was heavily neglected by the South African Police, while minor political- or administrative-type offenses, such as not being in possession of the right pass in a white area and transgressions of racial frontiers, were policed with rigor.[39]

Such different priorities also shaped the politics of statistics in the different regimes: "Black on black crime" literally did not count, because "blacks did not count," since they were not conceived as belonging to the South African nation.[40] Before 1994 national crime data excluded crimes that were reported in the "autonomous" and "self-governing" territories.[41] Evidence suggests, however, that violent crime was very high in black areas and constantly on the rise.[42] Up until the mid-1980s the government successfully sealed off black areas and made white areas widely unaffected by the crime taking place elsewhere. Against the background of apartheid politics of containing trouble, it is not surprising that the manager could walk on the beach before 1994 without fear. Yet, the facts discussed above give his lost freedom a different spin. The "sudden explosion" of violent crime is to be read rather as a spillover of high levels of violent crime to white areas that had long been the norm in black neighborhoods.[43]

Not only were crime and violence in black areas largely neglected and under-recorded by the authorities, they were also widely unreported. Black communities did not trust the police, and the majority saw no reason to report crime to a police force that was dedicated to upholding apartheid rather than chasing down a township's muggers.[44] A 1975 Soweto victimization survey, for example, found high levels of crime, with only one-third of serious cases being reported to the police.[45] In an interview, a member of the Department of Community Safety and Liaison of the Province of KwaZulu-Natal reflects on counting and reporting practices in the apartheid system: "Police were there to ensure that those that were oppressed, were oppressed, [and] stayed oppressed. . . . The crime that existed for those who were oppressed was not . . . important, it wasn't part of the whole program of action . . . [of] the government, you know? So of course crime was not high, because it wasnt reported."[46]

A final factor makes comparing crime and crime statistics now and then even more difficult: There was no national public sphere entitled to or eager to "talk" crime statistics. In John and Jean Comaroff's phrasing: "Under the ancien régime, . . . [statistics] did not correlate as a free currency of social knowledge, whereas today, crime statistics have become a standardized measure of disorder, marking out a new emergency to replace those of old."[47] Overcoming the ancien régime's silence on violent crime is an integral part of the self-understanding of postapartheid democracy. It becomes clear that, today, when the beach security manager and many others want to "go back in the national crime stats" and "see the difference," they see the numbers *tout court*, while the practices of selective counting, reporting, policing, and debating that underlie their production are beyond their concern. This is problematic because it cuts truth into pieces and then looks at them selectively. The political life of contemporary statistics can hardly be made sense of without understanding the various past lives of numbers, stories, or maps.

"Racism versus Killing"

The security manager's statement touches on another provocative aspect in the representation and imagination of crime in South Africa: the question of race. With his remark, "We've changed this thing about racism and everything, but now people get killed," the manager draws a line, conceptually and historically, between racism and killing. Racism, in his account, is somewhat non-concrete and slightly dubious ("this thing about racism"), while killing is concrete in each single case, and its totality is measurable through numbers. Racism, if one follows the beach manager's account, belongs to the old regime and is replaced by killing in the new regime. Even if the security manager seems aware of the undemocratic urban sphere that apartheid constituted, he implies that this is somehow not as tangible and certainly not as urgent as getting killed. Constructing racism and killing as distinct categories obscures the complex ways in which they are entangled. Some of these connections will be explored in what follows.

A first factor in the relationship between race/ism and killing is that both victims and perpetrators are (and were) predominantly black. Black people make up the vast majority of victims of murder and rape, and both crimes primarily take place in poor, black communities, while white people are less likely to be killed or raped.[48] However, white people are relatively more often victims of property crimes than black people.[49] When it comes to perpetrators, most crimes are committed by young black (especially African) men—a fact that has fueled manifold stereotypes. "In the banal theatrics of the mass media," Jean and John Comaroff write, "crime becomes racialized and race criminalized. And both . . . youthenized."[50] The young black man is also the lens for police profiles. Several of my interview partners from police stations, private security companies, and camera control rooms in Durban were quite outspoken about what they are looking for: "black males between 14 and 22."[51]

On the other hand, the figure of the black male offender is "neither accidental, nor insignificant," as Posel, Hornberger, and Mbembe suggest.[52] The young black male offender is the product of a long and painful history of racial exclusion, racial violence, and racial dispossession, at present he is experiencing disappointment and disparities. This contextualization, the authors emphasize, does not lift individual responsibility from today's offenders, nor does it adopt a simple "apartheid-did-it" explanation for every brutality of the present; rather, it means simply to read the politics of crime within its complex historical entanglements instead of downplaying victim and offender patterns as being stereotypical or exaggerated.[53] Here, apartheid itself, where racism was institutionalized and perfected, needs to be read as a form of violent crime.

With 3.5 million people forcefully removed and resettled, thousands of political prisoners tortured and almost 20,000 killed in political conflicts, the highest known rate of judicial hangings, and entire populations harassed for administrative offenses, the apartheid state was a system of direct physical violence, a "criminal state" with "violence at its heart."[54]

Apartheid was a source and generator of crime and violence. The obsession with minor offenses and the strict rules almost by definition created lawlessness. Each racialized frontier that the apartheid state created coproduced systems of law and lawlessness. For many black people, the law's racially discriminatory face was an invitation to subvert it, and lawlessness, Posel, Hornberger, and Mbembe argue, became a weapon of the weak. Others emphasize the psychological and epidemiological effects of apartheid. Shula Marks and Neil Andersson have shown, for example, that apartheid created unbearable amounts of stress and tension in the daily lives of millions of people.[55] By uprooting families and communities and fostering a system of migrant labor, apartheid destroyed social support systems. It created a social order in which violence became pervasive—not only in state action, but equally in daily life—forging a culture of violence.

Since the state was absent as a protector and present only as a victimizer, crime was defiance, transgression, survival, and in some cases, worldliness and a valorized lifestyle. Gangsters, although victimizing fellow community members, were often perceived as community protectors, redistributors, and fighters against an illegitimate state.[56] In many cases, township gangsters became glamorized within their communities. As Henri Nxumalo, star writer in the popular African *Drum* magazine, reflects on the representation of criminals in his magazine: "Our heroes were the boys who could steal and stab. The more stabbing they did, the bigger they were. The 'biggest shot' of all was the one who had killed somebody—either with a knife or a gun . . . . These boys used to have a lot of money and were able to have a good time with the girls and buy them many presents. It was not long before I wanted to be a *tsotsi* [criminal]."[57] In the 1950s, *Drum* magazine had a five-year series called "My Life in the Underworld," highlighting the "adventure and excitement of the gangster-figure's opulent urban lifestyle." In 1960 the editors of the magazine selected, next to "Africa's Man of the Year" and "Girl of the Year," "The Thug of the Year."[58] *Drum*'s gangsters usually run *shebeens,* drive big cars, live in expensive apartments, and are acknowledged leaders of their communities. The gangster figure was portrayed as subversive, as "'courageous and clever enough' to prosper not only in spite of white domination but at the expense of it."[59] Criminals with their fancy clothes, cars, and trophy wives became heroes who displayed virtues of masculinity the apartheid state had largely deprived black men of. Thus criminals became "icons of a sophisticated modernity," whereas those who lived by the law did not.[60] In addition, the state indirectly encouraged gang membership by incarcerating millions for minor offenses. Between 1952 and 1962 alone, there were three million convictions for pass offenses.[61] In prison, many men, young men especially, were initiated into gang life.[62]

Crime Fighting, the State, and Its Others

The beach manager's statement brings us possibly to the core in the problematics of crime: the question of what is being done about crime. In fact, the manager linked his feeling of safety in the past to the fact that "there was still the death penalty. You know you gonna be killed as well [if you committed a serious crime]." In line with his fellow—otherwise very different—"nostalgics" of Soweto, he criticizes the idea that criminals have (far too many) rights with the present regime and are not effectively hindered from violating the rights of an innocent majority. Every now and then, politicians on the national level speak to this widely shared frustration and engage in tough talks. Jacob Zuma (who later became president), for example, debated the possible reintroduction of the death penalty in March 2008; the Minister for Safety and Security, Mthethwa, stated in Parliament that "there is no other way" to the crime problem than to "fight fire by fire"; and, at an anticrime rally in April 2008, Deputy Safety and Security Minister Shabangu was even more concrete when she demanded that police should "kill the bastards" (meaning the criminals).[63]

But beyond populism on the state level, what are the politics of crime in the new South Africa? Policing is fragmented and plural, and it was so for most of the twentieth century in South Africa. What has, in international debates, come to be labeled as "plural policing," citizens' "responsibilization," or "clubbing for security" in the context of a redrawing, weakening, failing, or criminal state indeed goes far back into apartheid history.[64] The police themselves have been a body of very different police forces for a long time. Each Bantustan (the "homeland" allocated to black people along ethnically defined lines by the apartheid government) had its own police force created as a satellite of the South African Police. The mostly black staff was trained by the SAP and was often officered by former (white) members of the SAP. "Homeland police agencies" reported directly to the chief minister (or the equivalent of the territory) and were known to be brutal.[65] The resources allocated to the officers for patrolling the townships were minimal. Instead of regular patrolling, the SAP would periodically raid the townships, set up roadblocks, and conduct door-to-door pass checks.[66]

After apartheid ended, a single national police agency was created that unified the eleven police forces of the Bantustans, or the "autonomous" states, as the apartheid government had also called them. If the new national police was to become legitimate, accountable, and depoliticized, it had to build trusting relationships with a population that mainly knew the police for its brutality and political partisanship.[67] The SAP became SAPS, the South African Police Service, emphasizing its will to respond to the needs of communities, and to be democratic, approachable, transparent, and accountable.[68] A milestone in this endeavor was the creation of Community Policing Forums (CPFs) in 1996. CPFs were to become platforms at the police station level to rearrange and improve relationships with the community through the regular exchange of information and shared concerns. The community was invited to trust and lend support to the police, especially through its intelligence.[69] In 2002–3 the SAPS introduced a sector policing approach, which linked policing to a particular territory and localized it, dividing policing areas into smaller, more manageable "sectors."[70] The SAPS thought of this approach as "policing as its most basic," aiming at encouraging the community to "take greater responsibility for their own safety and security."[71]

Meanwhile, many individuals, communities, or businesses in South Africa have grown accustomed to taking responsibility for their own lives as well as for their families and properties. They do not need to be given responsibility by the state or invited to be part of crime prevention (i.e., "responsibilization"); often the state's very absence or felt illegitimacy suffices. The yearning for a strong state coincides with a sophisticated set of coping practices that many South Africans throughout different classes have adopted. Opinion polls suggest that only 5 percent of South African citizens think it is the government's prerogative to look after them.[72] The landscape of security actors beyond the state ranges from private security companies to a wide field of community protection groups.

The different streams of non-state policing have their roots in apartheid policing practices. White communities from the 1970s and 1980s sought increased protection from private security firms, a trend the apartheid government supported in order to help free up the SAP to fight antiapartheid uprisings.[73] In black communities, vigilante groups, street committees, and township people's courts were common forms of self-reliant security governance in the absence of a protective state.[74] During the 1940s and 1950s, authorities actively promoted the formation of civilian protection services in the townships and "homelands" but later banned them for unauthorized use of violence and alleged political involvement with the ANC.[75] Various (illegal) civil guard activities emerged in the 1960s. Many street "guards" beat criminals on the spot before handing them over to the authorities. In short, the apartheid state failed to provide security for the majority of its population.

Security scholars have argued that the security deficit created by apartheid has not been reduced in the postapartheid democracy, and has, in fact, widened.[76] As Shearing and Berg note, "growing inequality in security governance has been associated with a growth of mass private property. Private constituencies are 'clubbing' together to collectively provide their own security through the use of the private security sector."[77] "Separateness" today is reproduced through markets, and the disparity in the provision of security has continued along new lines, toward a "market maintained security deficit."[78]

The private security industry has grown immensely from its earlier apartheid presence. According to the Private Security Regulatory Authority's (PSIRA) 2009 report, there are 6,392 security businesses employing around 375,315 officers, and the armed response sector is still growing: between March 2008 and February 2009, the number of active registered businesses increased by 16 percent, and the number of active registered employed security officers increased by 11 percent.[79] Kempa and Singh underline that the importance of private security companies not only lies in numbers, but in the fact that "there are no functions performed by the public police that are not also performed by private security organizations"[80]—from implementing road closures and check-points to private law enforcement, enclosed neighborhood policing, and arrests. "Clubbing for security" has thus a strong spatial dimension and is often related to the emergence of new urban spaces, such as City Improvement Districts, where policing services are especially provided for the convenience of business people and property owners.[81]

"Popular policing"—policing activities that promote safety and security without relying on the legal authorities—has also continued after apartheid.[82] The various initiatives under the umbrella of popular policing have different scopes and degrees of organization, foci, styles, understandings of crime, and conceptions of their own roles. Vigilantes, for example, are characterized by a reactive, ad hoc, and usually violent method of control.[83] As Buur and Jensen have shown, vigilantes do more than simply take over the policing tasks of the state: they also create moral communities and produce different groups of criminalized people.[84] The many different security initiatives, private and public, small and large, morally committed or simply pragmatic, community driven or business oriented, are nodes with their own distinctive interests, clienteles, and mentalities that widely overlap, but only occasionally collaborate. South Africa's landscape of security provision is a "motley patchwork of self-defense," intrinsically plural and splintered.[85]

In the context of such security patchworking, the regimes of handsome space and instant space are beginning to emerge. These regimes of contemporary spatial governance are the most recent configurations in the longue durée of responsibilization, survival, and structural security deficits as they reach from apartheid to today. If governing security and making spaces is a plural undertaking, who benefits, and who is left behind? What kinds of communities of crime prevention and urban subjectivities are forged in the collective and individual longing for safety?

The Politics of (D)urban Space

While the horrors of crime are the fabric of public and popular reasoning, the problematics of space are reserved for debates within academia, social movement circles, and, of course, municipal planning politics. Many sociologists argue that in postapartheid South Africa, class has replaced race as the chief ordering mechanism of South African cities.[86]

South African cities are experiencing a "new segregation," a "new apartheid"—based now on economic mechanisms. Despite wholehearted government efforts to reduce the gaps between the urban poor and the rich, South African cities, almost twenty years after political transition, stay "profoundly divided, segregated and unequal."[87]

While acknowledging the reality and significance of postapartheid spatial inequality and fragmentation, I believe the account of the new class segregation is too monolithic and needs to be balanced by the aesthetic and affective, the mobile and communicative aspects of fragmentation. Before engaging, however, in new regimes of governing (through) urban space, what is needed is a solid understanding of what the South African ancien régime consisted of. How was urban space governed by apartheid mechanisms, and how were urban subjects ruled through spatial means? Below, I lay out some core principles of apartheid city making through the prism of Durban, before turning to postapartheid urbanism.

Apartheid Spatiality

Governing (through) space in apartheid cities meant governing through restriction, separation, and exclusion. The apartheid city was a city of divisions inspired by an illusion of racial purity based on the fiction of racial distance.[88] While cities were, to different degrees, segregated in the first decades of the twentieth century, the National Party administration after 1948 systematized and sought to totalize segregation along racial lines. In Durban, African and Indian life was not that rigorously regulated until the 1930s. Industrialization, proletarization, and the stronger local state apparatus made for a gradual closing down of opportunities for independent or semi-independent work relations, freedom of movement in the city, and ownership of land and living space.[89] By the time apartheid was officially introduced at the national level, the Durban Municipality had already experimented with segregation and restrictions of its urban space.[90]

In 1950 the two milestone acts for the apartheid city were set in place: the Population Registration Act and the Group Areas Act. According to the Population Registration Act, the population was classified into different racially defined groups.[91] The obsession with nonmixing and racial purity was especially aimed at the purity of the white group. People classified as white were neither allowed to marry nor have extramarital relations with members of other race groups, while marital or extra-marital mixing was not prohibited between members of other groups.[92]

Under the Group Areas Act, cities and towns were divided into group areas for the exclusive occupation of a designated group, a strategy intended to minimize contact among different communities and create total segregation.[93] People living in an area they were not designated to live in were forcefully removed and resettled in townships and "homelands." For example, when Cato Manor, Durban's largest informal settlement with around 40,000 Indian and 120,000 African inhabitants, was declared a white area, residents were forced to move into hostels or to resettle in the new African townships KwaMashu and Umlazi or into the Indian townships Phoenix and Chatsworth.[94] Apart from the regulation of residence, the Group Areas Act also provided for the removal of other groups, especially Indians, from the Central Business Districts (CBDs). In Durban, however, a section of the Indian CBD remained throughout apartheid. Indian residents were no longer allowed to live there but obtained permission to continue their trade.[95]

Apartheid also governed the everyday. The so-called "personal" or "petty apartheid" dictated where people could sit, stand, buy a ticket, use the toilet, or enter a building in public space. Post offices, beaches, buses, train platforms, bathrooms, and theaters, for example, were separated along racial lines—either through different entrances or through completely different premises and vehicles.[96] Architecture and planning were crucial instruments in crafting such compartmentalized spaces. In planning for different counters, entrances, and waiting areas at airports, train stations, and many other buildings, architects also created partitions, contained spaces, and erected boundaries.

Governing Apartheid Spaces: Compartments and Membranes

Governing (through) space in apartheid can be described, in Fanon's words, as dividing spaces into compartments in all spheres of urban life.[97] It divided "homelands" from the "real" South Africa, townships from the "real" towns and cities, making them "scattered partial forms," as Mbembe writes, "hanging on to the state's body."[98] It partitioned beaches into white, nonwhite, and international beaches. It isolated servants' quarters from the houses of the homeowners and provided for separated public facilities.

This compartmentalization was a product of an ongoing process of "territoriality and deterritorilization" through the appropriation of land, the disassembling of older territorial lineages, the formation of new territories, and the creation of artificial enclaves (Bantustans, and later "homelands").[99] A wide range of techniques to mark and code surfaces was closely related to this process. Mbembe coined this "Graphism": a preferred modus operandi of the apartheid state, tracing marks on territory (i.e., through segmentation, codes, pass laws, separating and designating the use of land and resources) and on the black body (i.e., searches, floggings, imprisonment). Graphism, re- and deterritoriliza- tion, as well as compartmentalization highlight different instances in apartheid productions of space as a political means to keep racially de- fined groups separate from one another.

The compartmentalization of urban space did not mean total sepa- ratedness. As Deborah Posel points out, total segregation was the long- term goal for apartheid, whereas more "practical" policies were said to be necessary for the short term. This meant that the white city was not barricaded altogether. Instead, Africans whose labor was required by whites in towns were permitted to live in the urban area for the duration of their work contracts.[100] In that sense, the racialized frontiers in many cases can be more succinctly imagined as *perforated membranes* that allowed for a highly regulated movement between the different demar- cated territories under the regime of influx control. Influx control had a double objective: from an economic point of view, it was meant to efficiently distribute African labor to meet the urban and rural labor market. From a political point of view, it was to restrict the numbers of Africans in urban areas as much as possible.[101] Among other reasons, the authorities feared that Africans in cities, with their "traditional" social bounds cut, would be prone to propaganda, communism, and anti-European hatred.[102] In short, influx control was about administer- ing and distributing African labor, and restricting and channeling the movement of black people into white areas.[103] Fanon described the com- partmentalized world of colonialism (in North Africa) as immobile and the colonized subjects as immobilized.[104] In contrast, the South African regime of apartheid—a particular modality of colonialism—was built on the meticulously administered mobility of black people, since it de- pended so much on their availability for labor power.

By 1952 people categorized as African, Indian, or Coloured needed permits for each journey from a nonwhite to a white area to work or seek employment—these permits known as passes were crucial to this regimen.[105] Millions of black people commuted every day to work in cities or industrial plants. As G. H. Pirie describes, the apartheid political geography of the city created two forms of black commuters. The first group, the long-distance ("cross-frontier") commuters, traveled between Bantustan towns, where they lived, and metropolitan areas, where they worked. The second group of commuters made shorter trips between places of employment and black dormitory townships located within the city.[106]

Apartheid cities, in other words, were never completely segregated, but rather marked by a "dialectics of distance, proximity, and reciprocal dependencies among different races."[107] The figure of the black domestic worker in white suburbs embodies the co-presence of these different logics, as Mbembe writes. "Nannies" brought up white kids, cooked and cleaned in white houses, and often slept in the proximity. Yet, they were not allowed to sleep under the same roof; separate servants' quarters were built for their residences. Here logics of "interdependency" disrupt "the coded intervals of apartheid city." Instead of thinking apartheid spatial governance in totalizing terms of segregation and exclusion, Mbembe suggests the notion of "disjunctive inclusions"—a provocation that I will take on as I go about understanding new forms of governing spaces and through spaces.[108]

Governing Apartheid Subjects: Force and Discipline

How can we conceptualize these various mechanisms of compartmentalizing, dividing, channeling, and controlling in terms of power relations and subject formations? One could think of the apartheid urban system as combining a rule of force with a rule of discipline. Beginning with a rule of force, Mbembe's concept of *necropolitics,* which he builds on Foucault's theory of racism, is helpful. Necropolitics is a form of biopower based on racism, and it is a typical political form within the colonial context. In necropolitics, sovereignty consists of the "capacity to define who matters and who does not, who is disposable and who is not."[109] Foucault argued that racism is the means through which the sovereign power can put to death. Death, thereby, is understood in a

larger sense: It includes indirect forms of killing, such as exposing someone to the threats of death and multiplying the risk for death, but also
political death, expulsion, and, one might add, denial of the right to the
city.[110] In short, necropolitics is the "subjugation of life to the power
of death."[111]

It is in this context that one can understand Mbembe's description
of architecture and city planning in the years of segregation as "the
transcription of larger mechanisms of social and urban warfare" into
city making.[112] Race, even if it could not be pinned to a stable biological
meaning, was used "as a weapon in the production of a city of barriers
and asymmetric privileges."[113] This warlike aspect of spatial planning
and management involved the downgrading of certain categories of
people to raw resources, exploitable and, in Judith Butler's words, "ungrievable." In *Frames of War*, Butler argues that "there are subjects" who
are "not quite recognizable as subjects, and there are lives that are not
quite recognizable—or, indeed, are never—recognized as lives."[114] Such
populations are "cast as 'destructible' and 'ungrievable' . . . . [They] are
'lose-able' or can be forfeited, precisely because they are framed as being
already lost or forfeited; they are cast as threats to human life as we
know it rather than as living populations in need of protection from
illegitimate state violence, famine, or pandemics."[115] At the same time,
apartheid power relations toward such "ungrievable" subjects can be
understood through a second modus of power: a disciplinary regime
aiming at inspecting, supervising and regulating black people's work
ability, their "producer bodies."[116] In this sense, apartheid urbanism sub-
ordinated and serialized black people into hostels, compounds, jails,
beer halls, and townships. Such regulatory institutions shaped the lives,
movements, and habits of black workers in the city—always in relation
to the maintenance of their work productivity. In some cases, apartheid
urbanism entailed a project of "civilization" and the moral transformation of the African worker, as in the case of the municipal beer hall in
Durban (see chapter 3). These disciplinary institutions created "parallel
urban formations" that were intertwined with the city but always also
separate from it.[117]

So, if apartheid was one highly brutal, highly racialized, and highly
spatialized form of social sorting, how can we characterize it and link the
mechanisms of power directed toward urban space with those directed

toward people? The system relied on at least five intertwined components of social sorting—social sorting being here understood in David Lyon's sense as concerned with the question of "how populations are clustered in order to single out different groups for different kinds of treatment."[118] The first was the strict classification of people along racial lines and the attribution of concrete meanings in terms of rights, privileges, and possibilities to these classifications. The most important of those was the division between the citizens, classified as white, and the noncitizens, classified as black. The second mode of social sorting was the (often forceful) designation of people to areas for living and to compounds or households for working. Relegation involved a homogenization of social spaces (the suburbs, the compounds, the hostels). The third was an apparatus of architectural devices (partitions, walls, control posts, and gates) through which space was ordered, coded, and divided. Fourth, these frontiers and boundaries were clearly marked and heavily policed, though made permeable for clearly defined purposes and in accordance with clearly defined rules. Fifth, apartheid spatial politics was a regime of making (in)visible. Sarah Nuttall points out that the black body under apartheid was either "being made entirely invisible or being made hypervisible."[119] While inspection, control, surveillance, and bookkeeping worked to make black people more and more visible, the system of exclusion from the political arena and public urban sphere hid black bodies. Handsome space and instant space are shaped by and at the same time depart from those logics. They are part of a postapartheid urban politics whose features I sketch in the last section of the chapter.

Postapartheid Spatiality

Postapartheid cities set out to be integrated, democratic, and inclusive. Yet the postapartheid city is haunted by an "apartheid ghost."[120] Apartheid urbanism has left a spatial morphology that cannot be undone overnight, despite the efforts of city councils to build inclusive cities. As one Durban traffic planner put it: "Spatial restructuring is extremely difficult. And it shows you [that] if you really want to wreck a city, design it wrong spatially and they'll hardly ever be able to get it right afterwards, because it is too expensive."[121] Durban planners and managers often refer to the city's "dysfunction as people's place."[122] What Durban city makers mean when they say their city is "dysfunctional" has to do with the paradoxes of under- and overuse of the inner city. On the one hand, those who can, avoid the inner city because, as an architect states, "at night time, the place becomes empty of constructive activity because everybody moves out to the suburbs."[123] Such disbelief in the inner city is expressed by the often-heard sentence, "Nobody goes to the inner city anymore," or "Nobody goes to the Wheel anymore."[124] A drink after work? Durban's middle classes do not really partake in happy hour. Indeed, in the CBD after 5 p.m., when business people leave, the liveliness of the city leaves with them. A planner at the municipality, like many other white people, talks about the demographic changes in terms of "invasion and succession": "People moved in and then white people just decided 'I don't want to live here,' and moved out there. . . . And then, as the neighborhood became a certain percentage black, you found more and more people would . . . flee, you wouldn't get any new people coming in when people moved out, they moved out for good."[125] Claims such as "nobody [is] going to the inner city anymore" notwithstanding, Durban's downtown is frequented and inhabited by far more people than ever before. The former city manager explained in an interview that one of the biggest challenges for the city council is to make the city fit for its "new" population (meaning those who were confined to living in townships in the old regime as well as migrants from other African countries). For example, the beachfront originally made for 390,000 people (Durban's white population during apartheid) had to be redesigned for the enjoyment of 3.4 million.[126] In the 1990s, Durban was one of the fastest growing cities in the world, and urban management tried to react with low-cost housing in the inner city as well as with other urban regeneration and management plans.[127] Like other South African cities, Durban went through an extensive process of integrated development planning and infrastructure remaking to facilitate social integration.[128]

Among the ruins of apartheid segregation, new fragmentations have arisen, this time not directed by a state force but created in a polyphonic assemblage of private developers and house owners as well as a variety of informal initiatives and everyday deals. Driven by a deep fear of violent crime, the middle classes withdraw from the city into fortified cocoons of imagined safety in the outskirts of the city. They have given up on the city—an attitude that has further undermined the dreams of a truly public sphere in the New South Africa.[129] Middle-class urban life plays out in the mall, as Imraan Coovadia writes in his novel on Durban:

> So much of life, in South Africa, was conducted in shopping centers and yet one couldn't take them seriously as places in which life, death, love, happiness could be at stake. They were outside of history. . . . There were many such new centers in Durban. You could be sealed inside Musgrave, La Lucia Mall, The Wheel, The Pavilion, or Gateway for a lifetime. During this lifetime you wouldn't bleed. You would not suffer. You would not age a day, or live a minute.[130]

Coovadia calls this existence between life and death the "airtight existence of middle-class South Africa."[131] Others have described how middle-class residents retreat into communities at the edges of the city, with neither hope for nor interest in the wider urban public sphere. Dreams of a truly public space have been delimited by the fear of crime.[132] Yet, life in the cocoon, unfortunately, guarantees neither safety nor a relaxed life. In a "portrait" of Johannesburg, author Ivan Vladislavic depicts the arming practices of ordinary suburbanites:

> When a house has been alarmed, it becomes explosive. It must be armed and disarmed several times a day. . . . There are no leisurely departures: there is no time for second thoughts, for taking a scarf from the hook behind the door, for checking that the answering machine is on, for a final look in the mirror. . . . There are no savoured homecomings either: you do not unwind into such a house, kicking off your shoes, breathing the familiar air. Every departure is precipitate, every arrival is a scraping-in.[133]

Without much pity for the middle classes not breathing freely in their panic capsules, critics of postapartheid urbanism have deplored its neoliberal, privatized character and the exclusionary urban forms it engenders. New urban forms in South African cities, from City Improvement Districts to priority development precincts, these critics argue, are driven by big companies, or municipalities that reconfigure themselves as companies ("Municipality Inc.")—and they flourish at the cost of possible social and spatial integration.[134] At the heart of the analysis lies the emergence of a new segregation, as political economist and activist

Patrick Bond writes: "The reality is that South Africa has witnessed the replacement of racial apartheid with what is increasingly referred to as class apartheid—systemic underdevelopment and segregation of the oppressed majority through structured economic, political, and cultural practices."[135] This new class segregation reduces the achievements of universal citizenship in the New South Africa to a "contingent practice," where the urban poor cannot benefit from their abstract right to the city.[136] Most analyses of a new segregation focus on the social and political effects of boundaries, restriction, and forceful exclusion, and they scrutinize the agency of big business, the municipality, and their various partnerships. They discover, as it were, apartheid's little brother in contemporary techniques of urban politics. I argue that this perspective is too narrow: this framing of neoliberal segregation prevents addressing some of the equally important dynamics of urban governance. It not only fails to do justice to genuine municipal attempts of democratic und socially fair urban reordering, but it is blind to the manifold (if sometimes small-scale and informal) techniques of governance that do not speak the brutal language of exclusion. In this present phase of late capitalism, seduction and desire are often more powerful mechanisms of urban ordering than restriction and prohibition alone.

Thus, in the course of this book, I begin to spell out how postapartheid spatialities engender new dynamics of spatial fragmentation that are neither the direct impact of apartheid spatiality only nor reducible to contemporary "neoliberal city making," but are mixed up with well-intended attempts to build integrated cities and are expressed through softer, more communicative, and inclusive forms. The challenge for an analysis of contemporary security governance in a city postapartheid is to understand what new forms of social sorting have emerged after "disjunctive inclusion": if we do not embrace the totalizing diagnosis of "new class apartheid," and if we join Mbembe in questioning the idea that all apartheid did was keep groups apart, how can we grasp more complex dynamics of fragmentation? How can we rethink the nature of fragmentation as less geographically fixed and more affective and aesthetic, technologically dependent and mobile? And in what sense is the communication of what is allowed and prohibited different? If fences, "whites only" signs, and pass controls stated unambiguously who was and was not allowed to enter a place, in what sense have the guardians of different "bubbles of governance" reinvented the toolbox of spatial governance, (i.e., by paying attention to the aesthetic—inviting rather than excluding communications through space)? The regimes of handsome and instant space provide two answers to this conundrum of post-apartheid spatial governance. They are not the only imaginable regimes, but their intimate relationship with apartheid's ruins and their ongoing struggle to outgrow them give us a particularly valuable glimpse into the making and remaking of troubled urban spaces.

2

Seeing Like a City
Conceptual Devices

What we call security in the contemporary world is arguably an ideal wrapped in layers. To get to its core then, or, put differently, to expose it in emperor fashion, it has to be stripped: we have to work through its layers. Such a procedure involves tracing the techniques and strategies applied in its name and constitutes an effort to understand just what makes up a threat, a nuisance, a risk, or a crime at a particular moment in time and place. From there, major structural changes affecting cities worldwide may be observed and contextualized. Yet these layers of techniques enveloping security are not merely superficial. Rather, they form and deform the concept's imagined core so much so that they may never be stripped completely. Hence, there's no getting to the thing—called security—itself.[1] And, perhaps, its nakedness reveals no more than the layers themselves. The spatial life of security, as I conceptualize it, happens in those layers.

This chapter develops a number of devices for analyzing security's layers in their spatial manifestations. It is as much an investigation of the concept of security as it is one of the city itself, asking what makes the urban such a particular scale in the analysis of governance but without taking for granted that there is a thing that we can call urban governance. What happens, I ask, when we free governance from its straightjacket of "the state" or even "the city" and apply it to a heterogeneous landscape of "bubbles of governance"? The chapter thus develops a conceptual yet hands-on approach for working with the slippery notions of security, governing, and the urban. It makes the case for breaking down what

Valverde has called "seeing like a city" into a variety of bubbles of security governance and explains how I am peering into these bubbles—notably through "low status" expert knowledge and "epistemic wallpaper."[2] Finally, I weave those thoughts together into my frame of regimes of spatial security governance.

SECURITY: NEVER NAKED

This pursuit of security begins with what Foucault called problematization. Any process of governing a "criminal act" or an "unruly area" is preceded or accompanied by a framing of why and how a particular problem requires attention.[3] As Rose and Valverde explain, "Problematization . . . is a way in which experience is offered to thought in the form of a problem requiring attention. . . . As an example, it is now commonplace to ask how 'the law' regulates sexuality. But we would rather like to ask how does a particular problem—say that of homosexual relations or prostitution—come to emerge as a target for government, and what is the role played by legal institutions, functionaries, and calculations in this?"[4] Problematizations do the work of articulating a problem, a threat, or a security hazard that the actual practices of government can plug into. Government, as Foucault teaches us, cannot be equalized with a state apparatus, legislation, or sovereignty.[5] Instead, government as a set of practices and rationalities aims to shape, guide, or affect the conduct of others and that of one's self.[6] This can involve laws and prohibitions, norms and incitements, architectural design and technical innovations. For grasping the entanglement of mentalities and rationalities of rule with concrete practices and technologies, Foucault's notion of governmentality offers itself as an analytical toolbox. It focuses on the *how* of governance (its arts and techniques) instead of the *why* (its goals, interests, and values); it draws on the *effects* of power rather than the *interests*.[7]

Those effects reach beyond governing "security" itself. In fact, all sorts of other areas of public life are governed "through security" or "through crime," especially in situations where the concern with security is pervasive (i.e., the U.S. war against terror, or the widespread South African fear of violent crime), leading to a "dissemination of security rationales to areas of life far removed from both terrorism and crime."[8] Crime becomes "a way of making up the world so as to make it governable in particular ways, . . . a way of problematizing the world and hence of governing it."[9]

The imagined core called security, wrapped by problematizations of crime and strategies to combat it is, then, not the only field governed and nurtured. The practices employed in the name of security also affect other spheres of life and politics. They unfold in classifications and subjectivations that structure politics and everyday life often beyond the assumed core domain of "security."[10] They categorize people into "criminals," "prostitutes," or "victims";[11] they classify places into "dangerous," "no-go-zones," or "safe"; they cluster populations "in order to single out different groups for different kinds of treatment."[12] Such categorizations have concrete effects on what different people can (and think they can) do in a city and what they can't, who can move freely and who cannot, and who is excluded or feels unwelcome in a particular place.[13]

I therefore ground my "search of security" in an investigation of the strategies and practices through which security is governed, the problematizations that brought a particular person, place, behavior, or group into governmental focus, and their effects on other spheres of urban life and governance. Consequently, I do not use an a priori conception of security but follow the practitioners of security and establish a view assembled by their day-to-day approaches. Security is the way it is practiced and articulated; understanding how this gets done is the endeavor of the book, rather than its starting point.

THE URBAN SCALE

The analysis of security governance has followed certain "scale habits,"[14] namely, seeing the provision of security as a task of the state. For a long time the Leviathan—and its ghost—was the focus of security scholarship. This resulted in blindness to developments taking place beyond this assumed center.[15] In the past few decades, however, policing and governance scholarship has developed a fresh approach to address and analyze the pluralization of governance. The use of the term "policing" reflects this shift. Policing came to be understood as an activity not reserved to *the police* but as "organized forms of order-maintenance, peacekeeping, rule of law enforcement, crime investigation and prevention and other forms of investigation and information-brokering."[16] Indeed, concepts such as "plural policing,"[17] "multi-choice policing,"[18] "polycentric governance,"[19] "oligopolies of violence,"[20] "nodal governance,"[21] and, from a different theoretical position, "assemblages"[22] form an emerging body of thought in which the state is not given conceptual priority in the analysis of security governance. The assumption these concepts share is that planning, organizing, and providing security is increasingly done by a multiplicity of actors and therefore requires analytical tools able to operate with political entities other than state governments.

Cities are laboratories of such complex and plural arrangements of security governance. "Local relations of security . . . are not simply smaller, or even more informal versions of state level relations" but have distinctive singularities.[23] They are pragmatic and use various regulatory techniques stemming from different provenances and sometimes contradictory logics.[24] Older forms of governance are rarely simply replaced by more recent ones but survive and "constantly pop up anew in municipal law and regulation." Seeing like a city describes such a "flexible relation between knowledges" in the management of urban disorder; it is intrinsically heterogeneous in terms of actors, logics, and techniques.[25] For example, many cities have different police forces, for example, a city police and a national police, with both being complemented—and in South Africa outnumbered—by various private security companies as well as a variety of other actors who commit their careers, labor hours, networks, or money trying to make the city safer. The city is a site in which different projects of ordering overlap, compete with one another, and produce tradeoffs in a complex landscape of spatiogovernmental formations—from City Improvement Districts to shopping complexes, or from gated communities to vigilante action. Beyond those juxtaposing rationalities and agencies of ordering in the city, I want to touch on four other facets of the urban scale that mark it as special in the analysis of security governance.

First, cities have always been sites of nightmares about crime, disorder, and moral decay, especially around urban "underclasses," strangers, and the poor.[26] Since early industrialization in Europe and elsewhere, urban governors of all sorts saw the crowdedness of cities as hotbeds of illness and immorality. While the countryside was constructed as healthy, the city was seen as a place that turned good people bad—both through its physical conditions of overcrowding in slums and through its seductions, which villagers had difficulties withstanding.

Second, cities have been breeding sites for innovation, change, and invention due to their openness to external influences, and to the intersections and interactions they enable.[27] In cities, new trends are shaped and new knowledge travels between them through everyday global flows of circulation.[28] Cities are involved in different kinds of worlding experiments—from the ambitious "arts of being global" of aspiring world-class cities to the less glamorous but no less inventive attempts of urbanites to reach out to urban elsewheres in an effort to maximize the resources for survival.[29] The experiments and innovations do not always arise from high-level planning but often result from pragmatism and an inclination for "antitheoretical," "creative, dynamic, hybrid, open-ended knowledges" that inform the decisions and activities of urban practitioners and the many learning assemblages of urban inhabitants.[30]

Third, cities have been the places where urban planners and security strategists use and shape the built environment in order to produce desired political and social effects. Haussmanian boulevards to tame the masses, Newman's design formulas to undermine crime, zoning laws or apartheid segregation—the very spatiality of the city offered itself to a variety of regulatory projects.[31] Cities' architectural arrangements and complex infrastructures make them prime sites for governance strategies that address spaces in order to shape human behavior. They are thus playgrounds of spatial governmentality—the regulatory mechanisms that target spaces rather than persons (directly) to govern human behavior.[32] They are the sites where the uses and meanings of urban space are constantly renegotiated and fought over.

Fourth, cities are privileged sites for considering and manifesting contemporary "renegotiations of citizenship."[33] The emergence of new sorts of places with hybrid property-governance relations allows for new mélanges of ordering and multiple crisscrossing memberships. "New games of citizenship" are played in their various forms and call to be reincorporated into a political theory of enrollment and participation, self-government, and survival.[34] Not only is citizenship as status negotiated here, but also the different opportunities and necessities for citizenship *in action*.[35] This means asking for the many ways in which people "do the work of the city" and open or close spaces for collective maneuvering.[36]

Seeing like a city, with its experiments in plural and spatial governance, its nightmares and innovations, and its practices of citizenship, is an attempt to reformulate the conditions of the governance of security as they apply to the urban. But if "seeing like a city" is so much more spatially differentiated and messier than "seeing like a state," perhaps we need a more dynamic and detailed understanding of those different acts of seeing; we need to zoom in and understand the bubble.

Bubbles of Governance and Their Regimes

I suggest the imaginary of the bubble to get at a more nuanced and dynamic understanding of security governance in the city. Shearing and Wood use the term "bubble of governance" to describe different sorts of "communal spaces" such as shopping malls or Business Improvement Districts, in which usually more affluent people are able to extend service provision. These luxury bubbles are often not accessible to poorer people, whose limited abilities of consumption disqualify them from the status of "denizen" in these areas;[37] they are often "left to live and work in spaces surrounding the bubbles."[38]

Here, I extend Shearing and Wood's understanding of a bubble of governance, but unlike their meaning of the concept, my "bubbles" do not necessarily mark areas of privileged service provision. Rather, I understand all regulatory regimes of particular space-times as bubbles of governance. A bubble is then not necessarily a privileged space but an articulated chronotope of attention and regulation in the city. Chronotopes, as borrowed from the Russian cultural theorist Mikhail Bakhtin, are space-times, or time-specific spatialities.[39] In the case of security governance, the urban chronotope receives particular attention with the objective of making it safer.

In my reflections on spatial security governance, the notion of "bubbles of governance" is particularly helpful for at least four reasons. First, it frames security mechanisms in its spatiotemporal setting. Much of the literature revolving around urban fragmentation disregards the temporal aspects of urban formations, yet as Valverde points out, "each space appears to us not abstractly but rather embedded in a particular temporality. . . . Our urban environment is thus best regarded as made up by chronotopes rather than as made up only of spaces."[40] Space without time does not exist. The bubble, speaking in accordance with Doreen Massey, is an "event of place." What is special about place, Massey explains, is precisely that throwntogetherness, the unavoidable challenge of negotiating a here-and-now (itself drawing on a history and a geography of thens and theres); and a negotiation, which must take place within and between both human and nonhuman.[41] Thinking of the temporality of the bubble also allows for a more nuanced understanding of the emergence and lifespan of governmental projects. For example, some bubbles might move safely through the Durban "securisphere" for decades, while others burst a few days or months after they have been created.[42]

Second, the notion of a bubble of governance can help us trace how a particular place in time related to certain activities becomes a target for concern and regulation, either because it is dangerous or prestigious or both. It is important to note that the identification of a dangerous space-time is in itself part of such governing processes. Particular places become "imbued with a sense of danger,"[43] while others might be regarded as safe, or perhaps as unsafe, but less important. Spaces (of security governance) are "produced" when chronotopes of danger or priority are articulated, administered, or policed—whether well-equipped and staffed, involved in ongoing improvisation and struggle, with loud announcements and shiny advertisements, or with more implicit ways of making themselves known.

Third, the analysis of bubbles of governance allows for a heterogeneity of spatial formations in an analysis of security governance: from major urban development precincts to informal parking lots or popular taverns. These bubbles vary in their functionality, scope, use, and atmosphere; they are looked after by different actors and have distinct demographic profiles as well as crime rates. While literature on urban segregation makes us believe that the gated community and the forgotten township, the luxury waterfront and the popular tavern could not be more distinct, the bubble as a tool gives us a chance to recast our common assumptions and see commonalities and differences along other lines.[44] When we take the guardians' and regulators' pursuits of security in their respective bubbles seriously (without "knowing" beforehand how they must necessarily differ due to economic status or location), we might perhaps find similar logics or even techniques of governance across bubbles. In other words, we might see common logics of seeing like a city.

Fourth, bringing such different bubbles of governance into one analytical framework challenges prevailing a priori distinctions between formal and informal actors and private or public space. Formal and informal regulations are often driven by common logics, and the effects of the rules a car guard imposes on his parking lot are often as important to security in his space as the regulations imposed by a consortium of developers in a planned priority district. Furthermore, by analyzing "private" places (e.g., privately owned bars) and "public" places (e.g., publicly owned buses) with the same analytical device, I want to question those divisions along the lines of private and public that dominant governance scholarship still applies. For example, with "austerity urbanism" haunting many U.S. and European cities, where companies take over crucial urban management tasks, it becomes increasingly difficult to disentangle what is and what is not public.[45] By focusing on the concrete techniques that (formal and informal) actors use to manage security in (private or public, or hybrid) spaces, we might be able to grasp some of the more relevant similarities and differences in governmental strategies.

The bubble, then, allows me to grasp some of the emerging conceptions and practices in the Durban securisphere in more dynamic ways. Seeing like a city, as I see it, means looking at problems of urban governance through a number of bubbles.

PEERING INTO THE BUBBLE

But how to peer into the bubble in the first place? How to grasp, in other words, the kind of urban knowledge relevant to contemporary forms of urban governance? In my empirical work, I draw on two bodies of knowledge. First, low-status expert knowledge, referring to the ways local security practitioners frame their work and interpret and create epistemic sources and technological tools.[46] The second source of knowledge is urban epistemic wallpaper in the form of texts, images, statistics, radio shows, and self-help literature. The next two sections introduce the nature of these forms of knowledge and lay out why they matter and how I gathered them.

Low-Status Expert Knowledge

Urban innovators and officials rarely just apply the law. Nor do they have a checklist of indicators of virtue, order, and decency. Rather, they creatively combine common sense, job-based knowledge, and borrowed bits from science. These "low-status knowledges," as Valverde calls them, are messy, creative, and pragmatic.[47] The kind of judgments that seep in when police officers or planners do their work cannot possibly be deducted from the law or the plan itself. Sometimes, "20 years of experience" make a police officer "just know" or "sense" that "certain people just don't look normal in a certain area."[48] It makes them "feel" they are able to discern whether a person sunbathing on the sand is innocently napping or has gone there out of necessity, perhaps to sleep, in the absence of a home. One activity is recreation and the other, depending on who picks you up, is "vagrancy," "rough sleep," or "loitering with criminal intent."

In this sense, the concept of low-status knowledge is different from the imaginary of a unitary knowledge surrounding much of critical discourse analysis that tries to dismantle the one hegemonic project, such as neoliberalism. Low-status knowledge searches for "small-t truths," not just for "the master discourse."[49] For my work, this has meant not limiting my research to a particular institution, organization, downtown site, logic, strategy, technology, or profession in security governance. Instead, I initially followed all sorts of people in their searches for security: from private security guards to architects, from bar owners to police strategists or community activists. Their work contexts and coalitions, their efforts and frustrations became the focus of this study.

In addition to conducting a series of interviews and attending meetings with these security practitioners, I attempted to find out what sources of knowledge, tools, and technologies they used. I asked about any internal communication that seemed relevant: plans and reports, correspondence and evaluations, professional guidelines, maps of various kinds, advertising materials, and minutes of meetings. Involving non-human actants in the analysis of security governance became crucial to my empirical research. In fact, over time I increasingly integrated sidewalks, colors schemes, cameras, bylaws, crime mapping systems, fingerprint machines, and many other nonhumans into my analysis[50]—not so much to find out how a camera actually interacts with a criminal or a tourist or how crime shows on radio programs affect people's choices throughout their day, but because I wanted to know what various city makers think about those relationships: how a security planner assumes a camera affects the criminal, how a bar owner expects a particular atmosphere will shape behavior, or how a car driver believes his membership in an anticrime database raises his chances of escaping a hijacking. In that sense, the two spatial regimes I develop through the course of this study employ Latourian ideas in so far as they are built on practitioners' perceptions of and practices toward nonhuman actants in their daily fight against crime. My perspective itself is not Latourian; rather, I wanted to see the "Latourians in action."

As Latour points out, social scientists have to find ways to make nonhuman actants speak and to hear them, and bring them out of their "secret lives." Latour suggests grasping occasions where objects become momentarily (more) visible in order to analyze them. "Specific tricks have to be invented to *make them talk,* that is, to offer descriptions of themselves, to produce scripts of what they are making others—humans or non-humans—do."[51] One of those tricks is the choice of moment, to be alert for shifts that take place: the agency of objects may become more apparent when crime statistics are released, when innovations are introduced, when a horror murder attracts media outcry, when the soccer World Cup is only a year ahead, when a new government is formed, when radical changes in the spatial politics of the city emerge, as has happened, and is still happening, since the end of apartheid.

The practitioners' tools are great third parties in conversations. A camera screen, a statistics database, a checklist, the liquor on sale, the chosen color schemes, or a by-law might become the focus of a discussion about what kind of correlation the crime-mapping program can create, what change of habits the design of the garden might produce, what crimes a so-called bad building brings about, and what a camera can see. Bringing the nonhumans consciously into the situation of inquiry makes the exchange of information more concrete and safer for both interlocutors. The interviewer could ask detailed questions that would otherwise seem unsuitable, and the interviewee could point at problems and easily attribute them to the tool itself. Lines of explanation often went like this: "Unfortunately we cannot do what we would wish to with such program," "Unfortunately the police are reluctant to apply the technology," or "The new law does not allow for this practice anymore." Sometimes my interlocutors chose to make the nonhuman "speak for itself," which often revealed important details that could not have been explained in the conversation. Spending time in the municipal camera control room, for example, and watching a series of videos of criminals being caught red-handed not only gave me a sense of how the control room operators collaborate with the police on the ground, but also provided insights into the operators' gaze, their priorities, and their judgments with regard to who is suspicious and what area to focus on when having only limited eyes watching a screen.

Low-level knowledge, in that sense, is the kind of knowledge in action that security practitioners employ and create when doing their work. From these scattered pieces of knowledge in action I began to draw the larger contours of the Durban securisphere.

Epistemic Wallpaper

Low-status expert knowledge rarely just lies there waiting to be picked up; rather, the researcher herself is involved in mining it. In contrast to this, public discourse is accessible, visible, and present to people living in, walking, or driving through the city. Public discourse in the field of crime control articulates itself through newspaper articles, radio reports, general statistics, or political speeches. It also becomes transported by social media such as newsletters, websites, crime blogs, SMS networks, or self-help guides. Such public discourse is more than mere crime panics. It mirrors and sets the terms for public understandings of "being safe" (or "living dangerously" to use Austin Zeiderman's term).[52] It formulates suggestions and priorities in the face of violent crime from planning the city to living one's life.

It is not always important to know who sends out these messages. The fact that these messages are in the urban public sphere and affect people's judgments and decisions is what interests me. Hunt and Hermer speak of urban "official graffiti" as the various "visible forms of regulation [that] act to mark, scar, and deface public spaces" in order to address their inhabitants.[53] Nigel Thrift's term "epistemic wallpaper" seems even more suitable for my purposes, as it does not discriminate between official and unofficial public urban messages but lends itself to including things like advertisements for private security contracts, public warnings, and crime updates in newsletters and crime warning shows on the radio.[54]

I spotted various forms of epistemic wallpaper walking or driving around Durban, listening to the radio, reading the paper, talking to people, and trying to understand the regulatory landscapes of the inner city. My collections of epistemic wallpaper from my research stays are necessarily very incomplete; they are subject to my personal sense of wonder and assessments of importance and certainly favor the more "colorful pieces" and the ones whose languages I understood. Internet blogs from East Coast Radio, anonymous tip-off websites from the police, or the city manager's newsletters are as much epistemic wallpaper as posters or street signs that warn people about particular dangers of crime. In addition, public speeches, media debates, and public statistics are all involved in defining the political climate in which the problematics of crime in the city of Durban is negotiated and acted upon.

Critics of governmentality have argued that it is superficial, naïve, and insufficient to investigate governance through the discourses, rhetoric, or surfaces surrounding it. Geographer Faranak Miraftab, in her work on Cape Town, for example, suggests that we need to look beyond the rhetoric of city officials as used on their own terms to discover what the real interests of local government are. Along the same lines, Kanishka Goonewardena has argued that we need to discover ideologies *underneath* the aesthetics of urban surfaces. In my work, instead of searching for an ideology hiding behind aesthetics or the real interests local politicians pursue, I am looking for political rationalities that are *expressed* through aesthetic attempts to make the city safe, rather than being *hidden* by them. In line with poststructural theorists, I believe that we do not need to scratch underneath the (somewhat fake) surface in order to find out about the (somewhat true) political. In *The Will to Improve,* Tania Murray Li warns that "the rush to identify hidden motives of profit or domination narrows analysis unnecessarily, making much of what happens in the name of improvement obscure."[55] Instead, she suggests, we should take the proposition laid out by the rationale we analyze at its word.

Mariana Valverde, picking up the problematics of surface and depth, argues that we should not assume that "truth is underneath, behind, or beyond what can be seen and documented."[56] Rather, referring to Deleuze and Foucault, she believes that the "surface" should not be regarded as the opposite of "depth."[57] Playing with the potential profoundness of the skin, she coins the term "dermatological approach." This interest in visible, surface effects does not assume that there are no causes beneath events or hidden political acts; it just "refuses to assume that what we cannot see is somehow more real and more true than what is on the surface."[58] It is a matter of perspective.

Achille Mbembe and Sarah Nuttall have argued that the entanglement between surface and underneath constitutes one of the defining metaphors by which to understand (South) African cities.[59] "In our view," they write, "this dialectic between the underground, the surface and the edges is, more than any other feature, the main characteristics of the African modern."[60] Surface and underneath are entangled when histories of labor and racial oppression are thematized through the lenses of new architectures of consumption and advertisement as well as through postracist fashion styles. Surfaces, they hold, also "suggest a deeper diagnostic," for example, in the way they un-write race.[61] The endeavor rests on examining what surfaces, cosmetics, and wallpapers can *tell us,* rather than what they can *hide.*

In summary, by employing the notion of epistemic wallpaper, I refer to publicly available and visible messages on the "urban message board."[62] They range from visual cues to written posters, warnings, and advertisements, from statistics and newspaper articles to radio shows; in short, anything a person is likely to encounter on her way through the city. Through the shreds of epistemic wallpaper and the insights into low-status knowledge in action I looked into a number of different bubbles and from there out at the city again.

CRAFTING TWO REGIMES

What did I see, then, looking from inside the bubble? The invitation of this book is to trace the logics of two regimes of governance that cut across a variety of bubbles—rich and poor, formal and informal, private and public. Here, I follow the understanding of a regime as laid out by Mitchell Dean. With a "regime of practices" or a "regime of government," Dean refers to "the relatively organized and systematized ways of doing things, such as curing, caring, punishing, assisting, educating and so on."[63] An analytics of government, Dean writes, will "seek to constitute the intrinsic logic or *strategy* of a regime of practices that cannot be simply read off particular programs, theories and policies of reform. . . . That is to say regimes of practices possess a logic that is irreducible to the explicit intentions of any one actor but yet evinces an orientation toward a particular matrix of ends and purposes."[64] A regime does not speak with one voice. Actors and institutions alike draw on a plurality of strategies for goals that might not be exactly the same. They have different resources at hand and operate on different scales of influence. They might compete with one another, or they might not be at all familiar to one another. But however different they are, they share a set of beliefs and use a number of similar techniques to achieve their goals.

There is a shared belief in both of the regimes I am crafting in this book: the belief that what brings crime about is intrinsically spatial (a bad building as much as a lack of spatial awareness) and what will remedy it is spatial, too (an appealing atmosphere of a place or a person's smart navigation habits). Yet, each regime has its own spatial logic. In the regime of handsome space the effort is one of affective and aesthetic rendering of particular spaces in time. In instant space it is one of navigating around spaces when they are perceived as being dangerous. Handsome space embraces the power of flirting with space, while instant space anticipates and prepares the many acts of fleeing through space. By deciphering flirting and fleeing as the crucial logics of my regimes, I am probing a different dynamic and hierarchy between the usual "superpowers" of critical analysis of spatial governance—that is, segregation and exclusion. The change is one of focus and perspective. We might then be led to ask what happens to critical analyses of governance if we don't allow exclusion or segregation alone to explain and interpret the emergence of new urban forms. Flirting (the attempt to charm until the social composition and atmosphere of a place seems right) always happens in conjunction with repelling and excluding, but it cannot simply be subsumed under them. In the same way, fleeing (the ability to move on quickly, to change routes when risks are lurking) needs an understanding of the ways in which people can dwell in the city, but it merits attention in its own right. By conceptualizing handsome and instant space from the vantage point of these two logics, a more nuanced story of governing (through) space can begin to appear.

The regimes of handsome and instant space capture something emerging in this postapartheid, pre–2010 World Cup moment in South Africa: an array of reflections on the need to reinvent space as a target of governance and a vehicle of transformation able to bring about change in more concrete, hands-on ways than many laws are capable of. This emergent something does not mean that older forms of governing through space are simply replaced. The regimes of handsome and instant space neither leave behind nor aside older, harder, more conventional, forms of policing. Rather, these "other" forms of government surround and seep into them and are in many ways involved in bringing them about in the first place. Without the pass system and the barbed wire of the past, the prison and the gated community of the present and the police operating the way they do, the regimes of handsome and instant space would not have the same shape—partly because of infrastructural legacies, partly because of shared diagnoses of social problems, and in many cases because of the will to be different or more effective.

The two chapters that follow will necessarily betray reality in the interests of making an analytical point. By that I mean that my ambition lies not in describing reality as much as to order anew things that are part of reality—in an effort to make a different point. Looking out from the bubbles turned out to be a constant analytic search for other bubbles with similar efforts and techniques, until they offered themselves up for assembly in regimes with something identifiable as a common logic. The betrayal is that the regimes neither "exist" as such in people's lives or in security practitioners' efforts, nor are they "distinguishable" in clear-cut ways from one another or from other logics of spatial security governance. But this betrayal of reality allows for an analytical insight into the many acts of seeing *like a city,* and perhaps into seeing *the* city itself. Here, governing is plural, spatial, and done by literally everyone who tries to be safe. Seeing like a city is then also peering into the city as it is seeking to reinvent itself after decades of dull apathy. The proposition for the chapters to come is that flirting and fleeing are both the essence of this postapartheid "seeing" and the mechanisms of its transition.

3

Handsome Space
Governing through Flirting

Cities in postapartheid South Africa continue to try to reinvent themselves. This reinvention works through a recalibration of what it means to govern (through) space; it redraws the contours of the fragments that fragmentation produces, and it alters the fragments' texture. Much has been written about new landscapes of fear, where those who can hide away from the city in their highly secured homes and communities do so. Postapartheid spaces, many commentators know, have become "patchworks of self-defense" that are anchored in and further aggravate the city's unequal spatial and social fabric.[1] Segregation persists, both in the ruins of old (racial) segregation and in the layers of new (class) segregation.[2] I want to argue that while being concerned with the persistent brutality of segregation and exclusion in postapartheid cities, we should also be troubled about something else, something subtle and "nice," as it were. City makers, in their efforts to allay the sense of fear and danger, have discovered that places need to look and feel good. A range of charm initiatives pop up among the electric fences and alarm systems, and their appearances pose new questions about urban governance and segregation. It is the new widespread and unquestioned belief in the aesthetic and affective power of urban spaces this chapter is concerned with.

When asked about his remedy against crime in Durban, South Africa, then–city manager Mike Sutcliffe reasoned: "Policing is the last thing I would spend money on. I would spend far more money on beautification, on ways that, it's a cleaner environment, it's a nicer environment, you see?"[3] We do not know if Sutcliffe imagines the relation between beauty and niceness on the one hand, and safety on the other to be a causal one, but he seems to assume that making streets, parks, or interiors aesthetically appealing can lead to the same ends as successful policing—security. He also implies that money invested in beautification is money better spent; in fact, it might even replace policing. Sutcliffe is not alone in his thinking. Numerous public and private, formal and informal initiatives in South Africa and around the world invest in the powers of beauty to make places safe.[4] This turn to a city's aesthetic and affective features is more than the supplement of broken-windows-style policy fixes. It is a rationale of its own kind—something that we could call, in Nigel Thrift's sense, a spatial politics of affect in the name of security. If, as Thrift argues, "urban spaces and times are being designed to invoke affective response," we need to understand how urban regulators imagine and plan for these affective responses, to what ends and with what possible effects.[5] This means equipping thinkers in the fields of critical criminology and urban studies with tools to read the affective calculus in contemporary security governance and to watch out for the sophisticated communication strategies and sorting mechanisms—in short, pulling security studies around an affective corner.

To be sure, cities have always been "roiling maelstroms of affect."[6] For a long time in the history of our cities, European and colonial, urban authorities tried to police these affects because they worried about their possible effects: the "masterless men" of early industrialization, so went the rationale, were seduced and corrupted in the city, be it by "loose women," liquor, or communism.[7] Thus, urban spaces were designed to restrict any behavior that was considered dangerous or potentially criminal. I want to suggest that in the beginning of the twenty-first century, the roles of space and affect as means to control urban crime have changed. What defines spatial urban management today is not the prohibitive, moralizing, or forcefully exclusionary techniques of the past; instead, the powers of seduction and atmosphere have gained pride of place and have given rise to a regime of spatial management that I call handsome: good looking, well composed, admirable, flirty—yet dispersed into myriads of bubbles of governance. City managers, in South Africa and elsewhere, no longer see seductability as only a problem (i.e., as that which makes people weak, and thus criminal); rather, seductability is now one of the means of preventing crime.[8]

At the same time, an astonishing shift is taking place in the ways in which the causes of crime and violence are regarded. While human vices and pathologies were the targets of disciplinary projects in the last century, I argue that today, city makers attribute the root causes of both good and bad behavior to space itself: badly designed spaces create unruly behavior, while well-shaped spaces beget well-mannered denizens. Handsome space is thus the story of unthinking crime and violence from the urban social and placing it right on the city's spatial surface.

Looking Back:
Pre-handsome Spatial Governance

Before I develop my argument about handsome spaces in contemporary urban South Africa, I want to briefly point to an example from a far less charming spatial history in South Africa in order to create a background against which the newness of such rationalities becomes more visible. While apartheid is certainly the most evident case for a regime of governing (through) space in its most brutal and exclusionary ways, I want to look, instead, at an institution that started long before apartheid: the Durban beer hall. At the turn from the nineteenth to the twentieth century, many Africans, mostly men from the surrounding rural areas, came to work in Durban. The city, conceptualized as a white center of civilization by its white authorities, began to change its character—as did (the idea of) "the noble minded Zulu gentleman of olden times": "Gradually but surely," wrote the magistrate of a neighboring administrative district, "he ['the native'] was ultimately drawn to our towns, where there is a total absence of restraint. . . . Lured away from his old primeval haunts and conventions, away from his simple surroundings and happy associations, he ['the native'] was thrown into a churning cauldron of folly, vice and riotous dissipation he was totally unfitted to withstand."[9] The city, urban authorities were convinced, was a "center of evil." So-called *shebeens,* informal drinking establishments, were seen as nodal points of vice, where home-brewed "Zulu Beer" and spirits were sold to black workers. In these "hotbeds of immorality," as a local newspaper branded them, men engaged in "drunken orgies" and ended up either in "faction fights" or with prostitutes and, what seemed to be the worst, became totally unfit to work.[10]

The Durban solution to the dilemma was to redirect black men's beer drinking from these unmanageable *shebeens* to municipally regulated beer halls. In 1908 the Durban Town Council introduced a municipal beer monopoly on the production and sale of "native beer." Since then, its consumption was only permitted in municipal beer halls; *shebeens* were raided and closed down, their owners imprisoned. As a report on the Durban beer hall system reasoned, the beer halls were meant to "teach ['the native'] moderation as well as guard against his acquiring a taste for stronger liquor."[11] Beer halls became the epitome of meticulous supervision and control; their patrons often referred to them as desolate and uninviting, panoptic "cages":[12] "The beer-drinking portion is separated by a wire partition and near the center of the room is a compartment with a raised platform and glass windows, which serves as an office for the overseer and enables him to have an uninterrupted view of all parts of the building. He is thereby enabled to exercise effective oversight and detect any loitering or disorderly conduct and thus supervise and prevent any from indulging in excess."[13] The beer hall was just one of many institutions concerned with disciplining and "civilizing" black workers in the city.[14] Regulatory institutions such as hostels, compounds, jails, and beer halls were to shape the lives, movements, and habits of black workers in the city—always in relation to their productivity, and, at least at the beginning of the twentieth century, also in regard to their manners, morals, and health.[15] Space, in other words, functioned as a disciplining device. Desires were to be tamed, channeled, and transformed into acceptable manners.

The new, handsome regime of governing social problems through space does not govern *against* seduction and desire, but works *with* them. It does not care about people's work performance or moral degeneration, but wants people's consumption.[16] It is concerned with managing microspaces and shaping the situational behavior of people in specific spaces in time, rather than changing an individual offender or healing a troubled soul. In that sense, the regime of handsome space is grounded in, but grows out of, what Malcolm Feeley and Jonathan Simon have called a "New Penology" and David Garland a "New Culture of Control," in their respective analyses of changing rationalities in late twentieth-century North American government.[17] According to these authors, the quest to transform an offender's actions and questionable morality that once drove disciplinary regimes of "penal-welfarism" has been replaced by risk prevention and pragmatic management.[18] The new penology, Feeley and Simon argue, "is markedly less concerned with responsibility, fault, moral sensibility, diagnosis, or intervention and treatment of the criminal offender. Rather, it is concerned with techniques to identify, to classify, and to manage groupings sorted by dangerousness. The task is managerial, not transformative."[19] The focus of governmental efforts has shifted "away from doing things to people to changing the conditions within which people act."[20] This new culture of control aims at "reducing the supply of criminal events by minimizing criminal opportunities, enhancing situational controls, and channeling conduct away from criminogenic situations."[21] What began with principles of "defensible spaces" in the 1970s and gained prominence through the "broken windows theory" in the 1980s in the United States has been translated into urban control regimes across the world.[22] The rationale is that crime can be designed "out of" an environment, for example, through "target hardening," through surveillance systems, and through an environment constructed to make any "rational offender" decide that this particular place is not worth the trouble.[23]

Critical criminologists and urban sociologists have pointed to the exclusionary effects of these measures, the aggressiveness with which they act toward the poor, and the categorical suspicion they operate with.[24] But as critics we should not only be concerned with the overtly brutal and exclusionary manifestations of spatial power. The rise of "positive," affective spatial techniques to govern the urban confronts us with new challenges, and these are what I discuss as handsome space.

Why *handsome*, then, as an attribute for this regime of spatial security governance? Handsome connotes good-looking, admirable, big-hearted, well-favored; beauty with a note of masculinity. Handsome men are fine looking, have nicely built physiques, know how to dress and how to speak up if necessary. When spaces are handsome, they combine their good-looking, well-built features with an ability not "to take any nonsense." Handsome is not the attribute of a passive beauty. It is powerful, active, and skillful, which is how spatial managers imagine the affective powers of their places—able to attract some, yet ignore or push back others.

All of this is not to argue, however, that police and private security no longer invest in disciplining, excluding, and patronizing. In the regime of handsome space, the flirty logics mingle with the moralizing ones. Handsomeness, as it were, has climbed on top of older criminologies of place, such as broken windows policing and situational crime prevention and has transformed them, offering us new ways of thinking about spatial technologies of government in contemporary cities beyond the wall and the barbed wire, yet always keeping their imprint.

If handsome space promises security it only does so for a particular chronotope, encapsulated in a bubble of governance. City makers and security experts focus on security in a particular place in time. Anything beyond that particular bubble is rarely of any concern for most guardians of that bubble. In Durban a variety of spatiopolitical projects with different mechanisms of governing security reside next to one another, sometimes competing, sometimes collaborating—ultimately building a scattered landscape of bubbles. So-called Corridors of Excellence, Urban Improvement Precincts, or Priority Zones stretch alongside and chafe against smaller, sometimes more informal or less privileged bubbles, such as informal parking lots, street corners, zones around cash machines, or hotel entrances, each of them pursuing its own security project. Thus, post–beer hall, postapartheid Durban has become a landscape filled with bubbles of governance, and we must wonder what it means for a society to tackle its drama of violence as hundreds of mini-problems, each residing in its own separate bubble, each being solved as its own situation rather than being part of a larger whole.

Though the spatial life of security in Durban is contained in each bubble, security within each bubble has come to engender all spheres of life: from color schemes to atmospheric music, from repaired potholes to happy tourists. Handsome space, more than a "reality," is a promise a place makes about its own security. This promise is packaged in flirtation—sending out vibes, courting the desired visitors, and anticipating the possibility of safety—whether or not those promises can actually be fulfilled.

To disentangle the logics of handsome space, I want to suggest two vantage points: handsome space as a doing and as a spatial relationship between the bubble and the city. The three strategies of handsome space as a doing developed in the core of this chapter are manifest in what I call Right to Your Heart, Happy Places, and the Ugly Other. Each of these strategies touches on one particular dimension of doing space: on communication through sensual spatial codes, on the creation of an overall well-being of a space, and on the elimination of those other spaces that do not fit into the handsome-happy-logic. With the diversity of bubbles of governance that I visit over this chapter (e.g., a downtown bar, an informal parking lot, an upscale development district) I want to suggest that the regime's logic is not reserved to particular kinds of places or racial groups or spatiopolitical arrangements, but a widely shared ideal and practice. I then take it a step further and think about the relationship between the bubble and the city. A municipal bus project in Durban called the People Mover will serve as a line of flight to think beyond the trapped logic of the bubble: The handsome bubble can serve to isolate and distinguish itself, but it can also serve to connect, and to spill over to its surroundings, working for the city instead of against it.

Doing Handsome Space

If we accept Gillian Rose's point that "space is also a doing, that it does not preexist its doing, and that its doing is the articulation of relational performances," what is the "doing of space" in the name of security, and what is its aesthetic and affective doing?[25] The notion of doing space refers to the multiple productions of urban space and their desired and actual effects on people's chances of being safe—using and accessing a particular place, opportunities for reading certain spatial codes, prospects of moving from one space to another. "Productions of space" also entail the small-scale, ordinary, informal measures, the "stubborn procedures," and the "idle footsteps," which de Certeau has written so powerfully into spatial thought.[26] Here, spatial theory corresponds to Foucauldian ideas on the working of power in its minor, decentralized, productive forms. Doing handsome space is thus a bundle of different actors' spatial strategies revolving around (or hope for) the performative power of aesthetics and the senses.

This section discusses three ways in which handsome space is "done." Right to Your Heart, building on a downtown bar's security project, fleshes out a particular rationale of communication with denizens of a bubble as placed in the hands of all sorts of spatial actants. Happy Places, drawing on the Disneyland-like logics of governing in newly emerging districts at the Durban Point Waterfront, analyzes how security management has become inseparable from the concern with a place's well-being. The third section turns to the Ugly Other of handsome space— the so-called bad buildings—to reflect further on the surface obsession inherent in the logics of handsome space through its negative extreme. All instances of doing handsome space share the fantasy that a place's security arises from its affective and aesthetic features (or, should one say, skills) and that governing security means optimizing them.

Right to Your Heart

Egagasini is a popular bar in the middle of the notorious Point Road area in Durban's inner city. The owner, a young Zulu man, has a sophisticated, atmospheric security project for his bar. He always "knew what kind of people [he] wanted," long before opening the bar. His plan was "to be expensive," because "I need that type of people. Because, if you're cheap, you're inviting the wrong kind of people."[27] At Egagasini, attracting the "right" people and repelling the "wrong" ones happens through visual and sensual cues. In the lounge downstairs (the bar's newest, most luxurious addition), the owner has arranged the liquor display as a way of sending a specific message: "For the drinks that I've got, like Johnny Walker, you've got five different types. . . . So, I cut the cheap one and then I start with the [more] expensive. . . . So, now, automatically a person communicates with the product and then he'd tell himself 'No, I am not suitable for this place, because I can't afford.' You don't have to tell him."[28] The bar keeper does not want to have to "tell people"; instead, he outsources relevant communication to objects in his bar, using the liquor for conveying the rules of the bar and the access to his premises. In fact, according to him, the liquor arrangement interacts with customers, who by viewing the display of liquor in the lounge are able to decide whether they "fit in" or not. No bouncer or barkeeper needs to tell anybody that he or she is unwelcome; they will soon feel it themselves.[29]

The deal about who should (want) to come in, and who should not, is made between the (potential) customer and a range of actants on the premises, including the liquor, music, decoration, and color scheme. His DJ plays jazz, not "bubble gum music," as he calls the sounds in other popular clubs and bars in the area. Jazz, according to the owner, is a sign of good taste and is intended to charm the desired customers. In addition, colors (especially red, orange, and yellow) "are most important, because they communicate with your heart."[30] The colors of his bar, which he picks, and then treats as handsome actants, can affect human feelings and behavior directly, without him having to turn to more costly (human) mediators such as security personnel. The idea is that gifted objects reach people's hearts directly. The dead lion's head hanging on one wall is another skilled actant in the ambiance project of the bar (Figure 1). When I asked him why he chose the lion, he told me that he shot it himself in the Zululand countryside, and with great fervor, he added, "I mean, [it makes] you feel great."[31] What kind of people like the jazz, the significance of the yellow and red color combination, or the message of the lion are not explicitly articulated. The bar owner genuinely assumes a universalism of taste, a universalism restricted, one might say, to the people for whom he has made his bar and lounge.

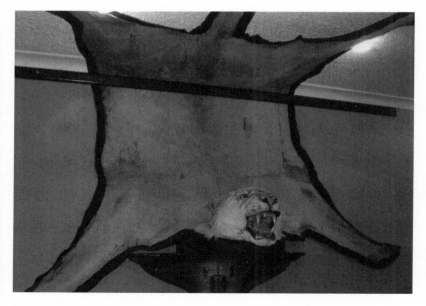

Figure 1. Lion decorating the wall of Egagasini, Durban. Photograph by the author, 2008.

In creating a place that charms the right kind of people through the language of liquor, music, and decoration, the bar owner has created his own spatialized "Lovemark." Saatchi & Saatchi, who have invented the concept of lovemarks, argued that needing, respecting, or valuing products are not enough—businesses must make their consumers *love* their products.[32] Consumers must be moved to discover the mystery and passion attached to products; they must plunge into the sensuality and intimacy the products embody. The Lovemark approach assumes that consumers make decisions on the basis of impulse and emotion. "Lovemarks reach your heart as well as your mind, creating an intimate, emotional connection that you just can't live without. Ever."[33] This concept is increasingly applied to the urban sphere, as evident in emotional city brands à la "City of Love" (Paris, Rome), "Charm City" (Baltimore), "Cologne is a feeling," "Love me, Love my Winnipeg," and many others. But we don't know enough about how lovemarks flourish in urban spaces on a smaller scale, and even less as a concept to govern security. Egagasini's bar owner wants people to love his place and be charmed by it, not just respect it. Ideally, he does not need to police people's bad habits because his place is skilled enough (it is emotionally intelligent, as it were). While earlier regimes of government worked toward disciplining and out-designing seduction and desire, handsome space frames them as something positive: They are the key to the safety of a place because they transport the promise of security.

In addition to marking who is and who is not welcome, these spatial actants of his bar are also implicated in shaping people's well-being on the premises and contribute to the respect they show to the place and other patrons. Egagasini uses its flirty surfaces to attract people, and to create an atmosphere in which crime is unlikely to unfold. While dominant "criminologies of place"[34] have created techniques for "outdesigning crime," I would like to propose the term *outcharming crime* in order to highlight the emotional language through which potential dangers are addressed. Good habits are imagined to proliferate and *outcharm* all potentially contagious bad behaviors. Outcharming crime, then, operates through a double mechanism: it beckons to the right kind of people, and it makes them behave the right way.

Egagasini's bar owner, just like other guardians and managers of urban places, draws from a wide choice of messages: flirtatious or repellent, coded or straightforward—depending on who he wants to reach out to. By doing this, he creates an "emotional field" that imbues his desired customers with a sense of being safe but also shapes the insecurities at the fringes of his place for those who are unwelcome.[35] Egagasini is located in a rough environment: the socially difficult and crime-ridden Point Road area.[36] The entrance to the lounge leads through an underground parking area that once served as a place where hawkers stored their merchandise and slept. The day before the opening of the new lounge in 2008, a piece of graffiti on the wall gave a clear message as to what was not desired in the underground parking lot: "This is not a toilet. No sleeping on permisses [*sic*]!" A meter away, another signed advised "Keep clean." It seems that the bar owner's flirty and nonverbal messages (to his customers) are limited to the bar's interior, while the negative and verbal messages (toward those who could constitute a problem to the ambiance or the safety of the club) are written on the walls outside. At the entrance of his bar, a sign says "no drugs, no weapons."

Figure 2. "This is not a toilet": Graffiti in Egagasini's underground parking lot, Durban. Photograph by the author, 2008.

Figure 3. "Keep Clean!": Graffiti in Egagasini's underground parking lot, Durban. Photograph by the author, 2008.

In addition, the bar keeper felt the need to talk to "the Nigerians" (who are infamous for drug-trafficking in the area) to make sure that they would respect his business and not sell drugs on his premises.

> I said to them: "Listen, I respect your business, guys. But never ever try to do your business in my business. Not even outside." I did make a meeting with them. . . . They respect that, because I told them that "this is my business and I am not scared. So if you come here, come and support me in a proper way." . . . Jah. They come and have a drink and go. They spend money. Because they know this is a straightforward [business]. When you do a business we have to be straight.[37]

Guarding handsome spaces implies the flexing of muscles. But these "straight" messages do not aim at excluding particular categories of people (homeless, Nigerians, drug users, weapon holders—provided they all can pay), but particular items (weapons, drugs) and forms of behavior (defecating, sleeping, dealing drugs). Via signs, the owner decided to ban specific *actions* and *objects,* not *people*—at least not explicitly. In contrast to older logics of "social sorting" in South Africa, which were built on the violent restriction of particular spaces for racialized categories of people, the emerging spatial modes of urban ordering that I am exploring in this chapter are more open, sophisticated, and subtle.[38] This renders social sorting fairer in principle, but requires an ability to read the codes, and to fit in. Sociologists working in Bourdieu's tradition have drawn on the "self-selection" and *habitus* preferences in the constitution and use of urban spaces.[39] People can sense the makeup of urban space, its inclusive and exclusive features, because spaces have inherent atmospheres that make their users feel comfortable or uncomfortable, invited or uninvited, safe or unsafe.[40] But how people perceive a space is prestructured by cultural, gender-specific, and class-based factors, by *habitus*. In that sense, German sociologist Martina Löw argues, atmospheres can veil the real mechanisms for inclusion and exclusion, operating through the access to resources such as knowledge, wealth, status, and association.

In spatial flirts, certain kinds of people are seduced while others are brushed off. What is appealing to some is not so "nice or cuddly" to others, especially those who are too shabby and poor—in other words, unattractive—to suit these handsome spaces.[41] On the other hand, for those invited and enticed, the beautiful bubble is also a form of entrapment. The logic of "lovemark capitalism," extending to the sphere of the entire city, creates an illusion of beautiful places as safe places and a fear of messy places as dangerous ones.

In this sense, Right to Your Heart as a strategy affects people's hearts differently. Ahmed has framed this unevenness in reaching people's hearts as the different "angle of our arrival." She writes: "So, we walk into a room and may 'feel the atmosphere,' but what we may feel depends on the angle of our arrival. Or we might say that the atmosphere is already angled."[42] Fragmentation is more than a rigid structure of spatiosocial inequality. It is also the line constantly redrawn between charming and outcharming, between inviting and disinviting people, between enabling and destroying opportunities, and between rigid and fluid urbanities. Here, race and class receive novel, more subtle and complex articulations.

Happy Places

The security of handsome space lives in bubbles. While it does not often reach beyond the limits of these chronotopes of attention, every light-bulb or bylaw, every builder or gardener within these bubbles is put to work in the name of security. Security is thought to emerge from a place's well-being, or as I call it, a place's happiness. Happy places promise security. And they do so through affective spatial cues. The bar owner's ambiance project is such a project through which security as happiness "is promised," or, indeed, flirted with. In this section, I want to investigate the relationship between a place's happiness and its security, using the "happy" bubble of governance known as the Point Waterfront, an emerging "world-class precinct" built on the ruins of the ancient Durban harbor area. Ahmed writes that objects are "happiness pointers, as if to follow their point would be to find happiness."[43] In our case, the happy places point toward security, implying that where there is happiness, there is security.

Point Waterfront is a fifty-five-hectare area at the tip of Durban, surrounded by the Indian Ocean. The land is administered and owned by the Durban Point Development Company (DPDC), with the municipality owning 50 percent of the estate. In recent years, real estate has been sold to private developers so that one day, so goes the dream, this place will become one of Durban's most prestigious addresses and key tourist attractions, offering upmarket residential units and offices, exclusive retail outlets and hotels, as well as a small craft harbor, a canal system, recreational areas, and delightful plazas.[44] With its aspirations and its taste for luxury, Point Waterfront establishes itself as a "city within the city"—well equipped, independent to a degree, and a place saturated with so much well-being that it spills over to the safety feelings and behaviors of its denizens.[45]

Once a Durbanite or visitor makes her way to the Waterfront Precinct, she need not worry at all. Getting there is admittedly difficult: "you are going through all the rubbish coming to a beautiful area like this," says the Waterfront security manager, but once there, "once you step onto our precinct, you feel the difference" and the difference is security—"everywhere you go there is security."[46] This means not only all sorts of architectural and aesthetic security standards and guidelines for developers and residents to follow, but also a melding of security, infrastructure, and daily management. Governing (through) happy places is thus a quiet, nonspectacular art that no longer draws a line between "security" and other features of a place's well-being. In the Waterfront Precinct, builders and maintenance workers alike are taught the delights of security governance: the Enforce security company trains them to recognize and detect drugs, and they are given radios to maintain constant contact with the security manager and the CCTV control room in the precinct to report any suspicious activity.

Blending and blurring security with the well-being of the Waterfront Precinct works the other way around as well: Not only are builders and maintenance workers expected to take over security tasks, but security personal must also perform duties that would not commonly be associated with crime preventing or fighting. After every shift, security officers must complete a checklist that addresses breaches of law, issues of "irrigation, plants . . . paved road ways, walk ways, street lights, . . . traffic lights, bins, litter, ablution."[47] They must watch for "acts of any nature which are unsafe," "blocked drains," and "any spillages by contractors or people in the area."[48] They have to check on builders and property owners to see "if they've put their bricks in the wrong place," the security manager points out.[49] Essentially, anyone or anything misbehaving in the bubble needs to be reprimanded, corrected, or prevented, because security, according to this logic, emerges from smooth functioning.

Point Waterfront can be seen as a development and evolution of the Disneyland logics of governance described by Shearing and Stenning in the 1980s. In their visionary article, the authors describe Disneyland as a place where control strategies are embedded literally into every fountain and flower garden, in every gardener's smile and in every sign guiding the queue. Opportunities for disorder are anticipated and minimized: "Within Disney World control is embedded, preventative, subtle, cooperative and apparently non-coercive and consensual. It focuses on categories, requires no knowledge of the individual and employs pervasive surveillance. Thus, although disciplinary, it is distinctively noncarceral. . . . Within contemporary discipline, control is fine-grained as Orwell imagined but its features are very different."[50] What began with the management of Disneyland, a private, elitist theme park in the United States, is now engendered in a wide sort of semipublic and public urban spaces. The Waterfront management in Durban also cares about their visitors' happiness—not because they matter as individuals, but because they are a part of this space in a particular moment in time. They are denizens of the chronotope. The Point Waterfront Development manager explains:

> We have like a contingent of foot patrol guards, along the canals and this kind of places who can also, they are not just security, they're also trained to assist somebody fall in the canal. They are like trained life savers. . . . 'Cause we're trying to run away from that old mentality where security was security and security. . . . Now, we're trying to go to another level where your security guy is basically an officer like a tourist officer, they . . . should be able to help you with directions and explain to you what the areas is about the monuments that we have, places of interest in the area. Like . . . what's the history behind. . . . That kind of basic tourist information, because . . . our emphasis is to make this place secure, tourist friendly place.[51]

In the manager's words, the old mentality conceived of "security as only that," while the new mentality of governing security implies making sure that the users of a place are there *happily* (and are behaving themselves, to be sure). The care for the denizens' happiness as a way of governing a place applies to other Durban bubbles, too: An officer from the Point Police station reports that he prefers driving around on his motorcycle because if he is in his car, some ladies from the Community Police Forum will always ask him to take them shopping and transport their bags safely from the supermarket to their flat in the Point Road area, a place where these (white, elderly) women no longer feel safe. A beachfront police officer reports on how "people call the police for everything: trouble with husband . . . the weather," and how he and his colleagues have jumped in the ocean to save lives, "even when it was suicide."[52] Saving people in happy places, in other words, comes in various practical, physical, affective, and moral shapes. After a short encounter with sex workers on their evening shift, a Point Police officer reflected: "But you know, they [the sex workers] get a lot of, how do you say, advice from us. Even when we arrest them, we advise them: 'Don't do this again. Try and change your life.'"[53] In the care for the overall well-being of a place, moralizing concerns fold into the otherwise so strikingly pragmatic and thing-centered modes of spatial management.[54]

Happy places can be upmarket, big, and prestigious, or more informal, small-scale, and ordinary. Just outside the Point Waterfront, Joe's empire begins. Joe is a car guard who is responsible for keeping an eye on parked cars in a parking lot in the Durban South Beach area. But he does more than just watch cars. The surfers give him their keys—or their wallets—which he keeps in a small bag on his body. Sometimes, he even calls the security company of the adjacent Point Waterfront to help car owners jump start their cars when their batteries have died. As a car guard who earns his tips by providing security, Joe has also created a system of good management, of trust and affection. Like the Waterfront, governing a secure parking area is governing a well-functioning place. For example, "there is no such thing as drug dealing anymore" on his parking lot, unlike "seven years ago when [he] built the parking . . . . They would rob people." Now, in contrast, "there is order, rules in the parking. No drinking, no smoking [dagga], no loud music, no begging, no selling the body on the parking. Even police when they drink sitting on the boot I tell them. 'I don't come to your job and do that to you, you got to have respect for my regulations.' They told me I am not their boss, but it's my job. . . . I know what I want."[55] This guard, who until recently did not even hold a license, makes the rules for his parking lot, directed toward would-be criminals and police alike. Securing a place's welfare not only transcends narrow understandings of security but also reorders the hierarchies of policing authorities depending on the place itself. Here both the police and the private security company are only allowed to do what he tells them. The parking lot is his bubble, and he governs it as a happy place of safety.

Security professionals, from police to private security to informal car guards, go about governing the *salus populi* each in their own separate bubble. According to William Novak, the *salus populi* was a core principle of the "well-regulated society" in nineteenth-century America, in which the polity was "responsib[le] for the happiness and welfare of its population."[56] In the "general pursuit of public good and people's happiness," the police cared for a wide array of aspects of public and private life, including preserving health, promoting communication, wealth, and commerce, as well as comfort and convenience.[57] It would be certainly exaggerated to see in the security bubbles of downtown Durban what Novak saw for nineteenth-century America, namely the police regulating "the remotest corners of public and private activity."[58] But the care for the people's moral and physical welfare as they reside in or visit a particular place resonates strongly with the care for the people's happiness that Novak describes.

When security guards guide tourists, or police officers bring suicidal swimmers back to life, we are witnessing a revival of the *salus populi* in times when the state is no longer the most important actor in crime fighting. In contemporary security governance, the *salus populi* is broken down into smaller spatial units and watched over by multiple actors. This also means that the temporal sojourners, the workers, guests, and consumers—in short, the denizens of particular chronotopes—are now the *populus* that is being taken care of by the security professionals. Likewise, policing professionals have extended their understanding of security toward the aesthetic, functional, and moral management of a place. Perhaps we should, then, say that they govern the *salus bubbli*—understood as the care for the overall well-being of the bubble, including both its spatial and human happiness. The managers, owners, and civil guardians, in turn, have extended their care for a place to include security. The concern with the *salus populi* of the bubble merges everything together—security and maintenance, happiness and handsomeness. This kind of well-being in and of the bubble is seen as the key to its security.

The Ugly Other: Bad Buildings

But what if spaces are too bad to be made handsome or happy? What if the place's owners, guardians, visitors, or inhabitants are indifferent to or incapable of making it handsome, or of caring for its happiness? Using so-called "bad buildings" as examples, I want to offer a counternarrative of doing handsome space. Bad buildings are not the opposite of handsome spaces. Instead, they are the negative version of the same regime fascinated with space and obsessed with surface appearances, drawing net lines from safety to beauty and back.[59] In the imaginary of the municipal and policing regulators, "bad" implies both the physical state of the building and the bad behavior of its users.[60]

Different experts from city councils, police and health departments, tourist and urban improvement organizations employ similar narratives to explain how a building becomes a bad building. Usually, bad buildings begin their infamous trajectory by becoming "victims of neglect in terms of maintenance by the landlords": irresponsible property owners abandon their building or do not maintain it properly, then water and electricity supplies become erratic, and finally, the elevators stop working.[61] As a manager of the Better Buildings Initiative explains: "So what happens is that the building starts to fall apart, see? You got all sort[s] of criminal element[s] that move in, you've got these drug lords that move into buildings—they then actually hijack the building, they take over the building and they hold people [for] ransom.[62] The building gets hijacked—a peculiar metaphor for a thing that cannot be moved, at least in the literal sense, from one location to another, like a car or a plane. This metaphor only makes sense if we think about hijacking as an action that moves the building from a good state into a bad one. The building is hijacked, in the sense that it has been deranged and thus transformed to its negative potential. The bad building, more precisely, is "hijacked by illegal people," as a health official explains.[63] And this, in the perception of the managers, usually means foreign African migrants: "The people from the DRC, Congo—they started moving in . . . and obviously threatened existing owners and tenants—ganged up against them and then slowly took over the building."[64]

Yet the story of the bad building begins noticeably with the building itself, not with the people—the migrant drug dealers, rapists, or thieves—who use it or abduct it. Experts and regulators have more interest in the derelict buildings, their agency and destiny, than in the people occupying or "hijacking" or indeed "pirating" those buildings.[65] The language employed is indicative here: Buildings are "*victims* of neglect."[66] Buildings "*have* prostitutes and street children."[67] Buildings "*harbor* criminals."[68] Buildings are "*sucking* energy out of the neighborhood or "take over the whole city."[69] Buildings "*are hijacked.*" People mainly come to the fore of the narratives as an illustration of how bad the bad building actually is or as a *consequence* directly linked to the poor state of the building: "Street children in the area then used it to sleep in at night and then people . . . broke in from the back. And they would rob people and run into the building. . . . It was horrific what was actually going on inside—a woman was raped inside there. . . . they robbed two cripple guys outside, right outside the place."[70] "Freeing the building," "protecting" it, or "turning it around," then, are the solutions these guardians of hand-some space passionately call for. Depending on the degree of decay, the building is "sealed off," "cleaned up," or "pulled down." The kidnappers are chased out. The Better Buildings Initiative regularly conducts "special operations," in which an operational brigade eliminates signs of illegal settlements in and around the buildings, such as sofas, blankets, and drug paraphernalia (Figures 4, 5). Attempts to hijack a building must be stopped in their early stages, the regulators argue. If it is not possible to rescue the building, then it must be demolished. The alternative choice of sealing the building is also an option, but this is not easy:

> There are all different ideas on how to seal the building: burglar bars, bricks, glass and whatever, but a lot of those things can be broken into again. The mortar got to set for twenty-eight days, before it hardens ready and they just kick it through. So we came up with the idea of just having straight flat metal, of which we just bolted to the windows, doors and front, back, painted it up and that's it. . . . Because those people who were there, have just been relocated.[71]

Whether the building is sealed off, cleaned up, or torn down, the solutions to the problem are always found in the spatial, technical domain, not in the social or political. We are only beginning to understand how widespread the spatialization of such social problems as violence and crime, but also homelessness, has become and what this means for a society emerging from decades of racial oppression and social deprivation. We also need to understand how much of what was once called "root causes of violence" is now sought on the city's surfaces. Urban governors and practitioners, it seems, find these causes in the makeup of the space itself and not in South Africa's complex socioeconomic reality or its history of racial discrimination, brutality, and exclusion. Handsome spatial make-up has become both the cause for an area's crimelessness and litmus test for a successful urban transition from apartheid into the future. According to this regime, if the battle for the surfaces is won, all the rest will follow.

The concern for bad buildings is thus an unease with "the ugly other" that challenges any ideal of postapartheid urban transformation toward a more handsome urbanism. It is indicative of the prioritization of the here and now (i.e., when it does not seem to matter so much where the

Figure 4. "Bad Building." Source: Better Buildings Initiative, Durban 2008.

Figure 5. "Clean Up Operation" in inner city "Bad Building" with Better Buildings Initiative, Durban. Photograph by the author, 2007.

street kids and other users of the bubble actually go when the building is barricaded or torn down). The bad buildings are also "the other" of the *salus populi* of the bubble; they are seen as places where people can be neither well, nor decent, nor safe.

A regime that holds its spaces responsible to such a degree is one that un-thinks the social question of crime, the historical rootedness and persistence of inequality. It spatializes and particularizes the urban social and political until little is left of a larger collectivity of responsibility.

THE BUBBLE AND THE CITY

The bubble and the city are involved in a troubled relationship that stems from the particular spatial understanding of urban crime and a lack of faith in the city. If life in the city is dangerous and this urban danger too messy to be addressed on a larger scale, the only thing responsible guardians of bars, shops, street corners, parking lots, or improvement precincts can do is keep their own bubble out of trouble, disregarding concerns with any insecurities beyond. If the city is dangerous and therefore a lost cause, and one can only be safe in temporally and spatially limited bubbles, then creating bubbles of safety must be an act of creating places. A safe place, according to the rationale undergirding handsome space, must distinguish itself by looking and feeling different from the city, and sometimes by projecting its autarky.

The managers of the Waterfront, for example, claim that they would survive even if everything else did not. Even serious issues such as power outages in the rest of Durban would not affect this bubble:

> T: [We are] buying a couple of generators. So the whole of Durban can go down, but not the precinct. You still have like your cameras [that] can monitor, [and] extra lighting for security. So it's gonna be like a prison, . . . put it that way.
>
> CH: Like a prison?
>
> T: Like a prison, where we don't miss nothing, we're like police wardens, if you're walking with the fishing . . . down the canal and there is power surge in the rest of Durban, we've got you monitored.[72]

The Waterfront manager has solved the problem of electricity for his bubble, so he considers this problem resolved. The fate of "the rest of

Durban" is not his concern. The city is imagined as an outside world, decaying, impossible to secure, and not to be associated with. The manager's enthusiastic association of his world-class precinct with a prison should then not strike us as awkward: In his world-class prison, in contrast to the outside world, everybody can be monitored; nobody escapes, not even during power outages. Here the dynamics of being locked in and locked out seem reversed. People are allowed to leave the precinct, but might not necessarily want to because they fear the world beyond the borders of the precinct. The trouble is more about controlling who gets in. As the security manager explains: "Obviously we don't want people with no purpose being here. It's one of the easiest ways to control crime, is to control access."[73] In an advertising leaflet for the Point Waterfront, a map shows a half-bird's-eye-view/half-silhouette of Durban seen from the Point harbor area. The area of Point Waterfront is framed with a thin red line (Figure 6). In "reality," the Waterfront does not have a visible territorial boundary, but from the perspective of both managers and visitors alike, this line is real. This is where the cameras of the Enforce private security control room start, where the security personnel begin patrolling for law and order, and where the security personnel push rowdy clubbers, vagrants, prostitutes, and car washers out of the precinct.[74] Preserving the bubble's integrity by pushing crime "out of the precinct" is the rationale behind this line.[75] Upgrading one's own bubble with the effect of "bouncing the problem back into the rest of the city" is a common, rarely questioned spatial practice.[76] Happy places like the Waterfront keep their beauty and smooth operation to themselves; the more prominent their handsomeness in comparison to the surrounding areas, the more convincing their promise of security.

While most bubbles seem to indulge in their distinctiveness, some are designed to make an impact beyond themselves. The People Mover is a new bus project for Durban's inner city. It is handsome, distinctive, and charming in many of the same ways as the Waterfront bubble, but rather than cocooning itself away from the city, it reaches toward the city and wants to affect it. Created by the Durban municipality in 2008, the People Mover is promoted on the municipality's website as being "the most exciting mode of transport to ever hit Durban's streets. It revolutionizes public transport with world class safety, luxurious comfort, and meticulous reliability."[77] In addition to being one of the few

Figure 6. Advertisement for Point Waterfront as "Investment Opportunity." Source: Durban Point Development Company n.d.

bus systems in Durban with timetables, the People Mover looks fancy—it is purposefully designed to be a mobile zone of temporal comfort and safety. Its website states that the "People Mover bus branding has been created to reflect the mood of Durban: tropical, colorful, coastal, trendy, laid-back and funky."[78] Its messages, conveyed through style, comfort, and regularity, are visible on the outside of the bus as well as on the carefully designed bus stops, many of which are guarded by security officers. In fact, one gets a sense of the People Mover long before seeing it or stepping on board. Its promise, to use Ahmed again, "sends forth" a sense of security—security that arrives every fifteen minutes, from 6 a.m. to 11 p.m.[79]

The People Mover attempts to become a "moving area up-grader"; wherever it goes, the area "gets a push"—not only for places that are already in "good shape," such as the beachfront, but more importantly, for the beach hinterland.[80] That is why the bus runs one street back from the (already upgraded) beachfront, right through Gillespie Street, which is right in the infamous Point Road area. One of the initiators reflects on a difficult discussion process: "People were saying 'Are you mad? That's gonna be mugger's paradise.' We were saying 'because it's a priority transport node, you are automatically gonna get security [to] prioritize on it and so that will just make the common criminals uncomfortable.' . . . It's all about reclaiming public space. . . . I think there's gonna be kind of cyclical pressure come on to it, which will start to turn it."[81]

According to its developers, the People Mover will slowly transform "bad areas" toward the better; it is, in the words of the former head of the city's Strategic Projects Department, a "regeneration tool": the mobile bubble carries its security concept as it moves through its environment and radiates its positive effects onto the surrounding area. The security guards who watch over the umbrella-like bus shelters and inform passengers when the next bus will arrive or wave the bus over for them are part of this security promise (Figures 7, 8, 9). In addition, the ten buses that operated during the first two years of the initiative were equipped with CCTV. The developer of the People Mover reflected: "There are five cameras in the bus, four filming the bus inside, and one is on the road. . . . And for me, that's filming the drug lords. The best thing to do is actually to displace [the drug lords]. . . . They get uncomfortable to operate in the area."[82] While the People Mover wants to charm its passengers, it clearly wants to "outcharm" drug dealers and other criminals. With cameras, guards, and funky chic conquering the run-down beach hinterland, the drug lords are meant to see the code of the area changing. In what sense the drug pushers surrender (if at all) to the handsomeness of the area frequented by the bus remains unclear, but it is remarkable to what extent both the bus and the bus stops have become meeting places for people who gather and wait to take the bus, claiming presence in an area that people might have otherwise avoided or rushed through.

When the People Mover started its operations in 2008, the buses were often empty, and when I asked around, I realized that only a few people knew about the system. Those who drove their private cars on a daily basis did not seem thrilled by the idea of a new funky bus with a "tropical feel," and those who used public transport tended to think that it was a bus for tourists. In addition, the 5 Rand (one way) ticket was slightly more expensive than the cost of the minibus taxis and other municipal buses at the time. Only a few police officers on their way to work to Point Police Station seemed to find this new means of transport handy. (Imagine the security bubble: cops and CCTV in the bus, security guards at the bus stops—who can ask for more supervision?) Since then, more and more locals have become used to the People Mover. In 2010 the number of buses increased to twenty-three buses. An additional line was created, so that nowadays three People Mover lines are running: the Beach Line (parallel to the beachfront from Moses Mabhida Stadium down to the Point Waterfront), the City Line (from South Beach into the inner city to the Warwick Junction traffic hub), and the Circle Line (passing UNISA, Durban station, Albert Park, etc.) At the time of my last visit in 2013, the buses were packed most of the time. The fare is still at 5 Rand, which is now the same as the fare for the taxis.

Built in a handsome logic with a touch of exclusivity, the People Mover has evolved into a more ordinary urban bubble. The People Mover is a chronotope that connects and opens up to the city, rather than isolating itself from it. It moves away from an exclusive understanding of handsome or happy and toward sharing a spatial optimism: by sending its vibes to the area that surrounds it, stretching the operational hours in which most municipal transport runs, and cutting through race and class-specific dynamics that exist in the use of public and private

Figure 7. Security guard at one of the original umbrella-like bus shelters. Photograph by the author, 2009.

Figure 8. New People Mover bus shelter, City Line, Durban. Photograph by the author, 2013.

Figure 9. Passengers waiting at People Mover bus shelter, City Line, Durban. Photograph by the author, 2013.

transport in Durban. A line of flight in the logic of handsome space, the People Mover helps us imagine the bubble as not always cocooning itself away from the city for fearing the city's contagiousness. The People Mover as handsome bubble is designed to be "contagious" to the city.

Outcharming Crime and the Handsome Bubble

As a litmus test for postapartheid spatial transformation, handsome space is disappointing. Its surface obsession buries the layers of violent crime born of apartheid.[83] Handsome space is itself an expression and reinforcement of a politics of the here-and-now. It is trapped in what critical criminologists have termed the "cosmetic fallacy":

> The cosmetic fallacy conceives of crime as a superficial problem of society, skin deep, which can be dealt with using the appropriate ointment, rather than as any chronic ailment of society as a whole. It engenders a cosmetic criminology which views crime as a blemish which suitable

treatment can remove from a body, which is, itself, otherwise healthy and in little need of reconstruction.[84]

To be sure, the regime of handsome space inscribes itself into Jock Young's diagnosis of skin-deep superficiality. But what we need to understand is something else: how the surface is not *just* the surface, how the bubble is not *just* the bubble, but has become the arena in which the social is negotiated and its problems addressed. Perhaps, then, what we used to call "root causes" of violent crime have not simply vanished, but are redefined and "turned up" on and as the urban surface. If we take these surface obsessions seriously, we need to acknowledge the degree to which city makers, security strategists, and urban entrepreneurs attribute the reason for safety or for crime to the very spatiality of a building, a park or a club. Badly shaped and disorderly places are seen as the root causes of criminal activities (accused of attracting or producing bad denizens and bad habits), while good-looking spaces with happy vibes are expected to "outcharm" crime. Surfaces are the new root causes, the here and now is the new horizon for collective action. The change is dramatic: it is not just the bubble, not just the surface, but here is where the social and political reside, and here is where we need to analyze it.

In the bubble, and on the surface, the rationales of governing are all encompassing. Where theories of Situational Crime Prevention and Broken Windows policing looked for approaches to repel the bad guys and reduce opportunities for crime—always appealing to people's rational choice—the protagonists of handsome space believe in "affective choice" engendered by the handsomeness, functionality, and the good vibes of their place. While scholars of governmentality have pointed us to the new forms of "governance at the distance,"[85] handsome space attracts our curiosity for a range of rationales that could rather be termed governance through closeness, or through touch, as Davina Cooper has called it.[86] In this direct and intimate form of governing through space, the security-relevant communication takes a shortcut, from the lion head right to people's heart.

Security in handsome space is a public good only in the measure of the bubble. It inhabits the time-space of a bar, a business improvement precinct, a park, or a bus and many other chronotopes whose security projects might be even less clearly articulated. In the bubble, security's meaning (and means) seems truly inescapable. Garbage collection, drainage systems, cars jump-started, and tourist happiness are all made to work for the pursuit of security. Through them, to adapt Ahmed again, the promise of security is sent forth.

Outside the bubble is the city, a decaying world, impossible to save, possibly contagious, and thus best avoided. But we have seen that bubbles can have different modes of being permeable, inviting, radiating, closed, inward oriented—and except for the rare bubble—determined to keep their beauty and happiness for themselves. Thinking about the bubble and the city is then always thinking about the art of drawing the line—between desired and undesired visitors, between implicit and explicit communication, between us and the rest, and between opening up and isolating oneself. In this sense the People Mover brings some motion into handsome space, since it so explicitly wants to be porous, penetrating the city's bubbles and being itself constantly penetrated by a mixed crowd of urban residents.

Practitioners and scholars alike need a vision to connect the bubbles, to see how all projects—be they small, elitist, or isolated—become part of some larger urban collectivity and work toward security understood broadly. Otherwise the pursuit of security in the bubble will always be, in Loader's words, a pursuit of security "that permit[s] one to disregard the security concerns of others, and to bracket off the effects of one's security-seeking activity upon them."[87] Here, perhaps, lies the true charm of the bubble: it can grow in time and space and responsibility. A landscape of bubbles can thus be different from a fragmented city, because of its potential to overcome its own narrowness. Bubbles can make foam.

4

Instant Space

Governing through Fleeing

In 2007 Durban's biggest public radio channel EastCoastRadio promoted its crime-monitoring program with a compelling poster. The picture displays an ordinary beachfront scene: blue sky, turquoise water, green palm trees, a few cars, flâneurs, and a white surfer. Only the big tank in the middle of the parking area disturbs the harmony. The text says: "There's an easier way to avoid crime. Tune in to Crimewatch every Monday, Wednesday and Friday at 9:20 am. Get the latest updates on crime prevention as well as useful safety and self-defense tips for you and your family" (Figure 10).

A tank, of course, is not a typical means of fighting crime in South Africa. However, it is a symbol of a bulky power, of an all too stiff and heavy-handed state that proves inefficient in the face of South Africa's crisis of violent crime. The promise of EastCoastRadio, in contrast, seems refreshing: flexible and easy-to-use crime prevention tools for everyone are meant to replace the ponderous relics of state-governed security from an "era of hardware."[1]

CrimeWatch on EastCoastRadio is one of many efforts to keep people safe by appealing to their own expertise in crime prevention. Numerous initiatives, from crime newsletters, blogs and self-help guides, to participatory crime mapping and cell phone services, offer their assistance to crime-aware citizens on how to be safe on their journeys through the city. Since it is impossible to permanently remain within the supposed islands of safety that the guardians of handsome space seek to create, urban residents must build their personal, yet networked, crime-related "navigation" systems in order to circulate through the city.

There's an easier way to avoid crime.

Tune in to Crimewatch every Monday, Wednesday and Friday at 9:20am. Get the latest updates on crime prevention as well as useful safety and self defence tips for you and your family.

EastCoast Radio
CRIME WATCH

Figure 10. Advertisement for EastCoastRadio's Crimewatch. Source: EastCoastRadio, 2007.

This chapter is about the art of navigating the city—and surviving. It is about the skill of circumventing dangers and "outsmarting" crime. In contrast to handsome space, where security is pursued as the good of a concrete physical place, this chapter reconstructs the longing for security in spatial and communicative practices of urban residents as they make their way through the city. Security, in the logic of this regime, is a situational experience that grows with a person's communicative skills, spatial literacy, access to technology, and involvement in information sharing communities.

This regime of security governance is instant: instant crime avoidance practices, enabled through instant communication, in instant communities. Like instant soup or instant coffee, instant crime avoidance techniques claim to be easy, immediately consumable, and almost infallible. They are solutions for the here and now with the promise to cater to each individual's taste. They are enabled by the technological innovations of experts, who have reduced a complex reality of crime and violence to a variety of simple avoidance toolkits.

But in subscribing to SMS crime information systems, anonymous crime hotlines, or how-to-avoid-hijackings advice, users can and do ignore the social causes of crime in South Africa. Far from understanding the structural mechanism of violence and insecurity, they learn instead the how-to-use-it knowledge to calculate and avoid risks, and by that, to prevent robberies, mugging, or hijacking in the here and now. For the "do-it-yourselfers," insecurity is a social fact that cannot be overcome—though it can be measured, visualized, communicated, and ultimately, individually avoided. The language of avoiding crime is indicative: the aim is not to stop the crime from happening, but to know where and when it is most likely to hit so one can navigate around it, this time, and then again and again.

Governmentality studies and critical criminology have long analyzed the "deflecting [of] former state obligations onto private citizens" as "responsibilization" and "governance at a distance."[2] As David Garland has argued, the state's new strategy is "not to command and control but rather to persuade and align, to organize, to ensure that other actors play their part."[3] In such rearticulations of capacities and responsibilities, the citizen becomes a specialist in the field of "criminologies of everyday life."[4]

The regime of instant space, on which I will elaborate in this chapter, engenders such criminologies of the everyday in ever more far-reaching and nuanced ways. In this form of governance at a distance, the state might be far off, but the techniques of governance themselves have become extremely direct and incredibly close to the technophile subjects of instant space. Instant space wants its subjects' best senses and prudence; it needs their permanent alertness and their readiness: for immediate response, for changing their plans, for consuming the necessary services and information. Its temporality is complex: instant space takes place in the here and now, but the immediacy of avoiding crime is inseparable from the longer project of surviving. In instant space, "governing through crime reaches, as it were, 'all the way down'—filling the minds and lives of subjects with a daily (and endless) search for security and justice."[5]

Looking Back: Security as Self-Care in Urban South Africa

Security as a personal matter is not without precedent in South Africa. The state has never lived up to the ideal of protecting its population from violence. This is especially true of the apartheid period, when the majority of the population were regarded as noncitizens, and therefore actively denied the state's security provision. Black people were policed for control, not for crime prevention, which meant that they could be imprisoned for minor political- or administrative-type offenses, such as not being in possession of the right pass in a white area.[6] The South African Police was mainly interested in "containing township crime rather than combating it."[7] "Passes and documents were checked, raids for illicit liquor conducted and illegal squatters evicted, all while murder, rape and gangsterism flourished."[8]

The state's under-resourced security provision for the majority of South Africans gave rise to a range of self-help measures—from street patrols to blowing whistles and using flashlights.[9] Two advertisements for Eveready brand batteries, appearing in *Drum* magazine in the 1950s, are particularly insightful when compared to the campaign poster for EastCoastRadio's crime bulletin (Figures 11 and 12).[10] The first advertisement depicts a black man wearing a hat, holding up his collar as if trying to hide something. From the bottom corner of the ad, another

Figure 11. Advertisement for Eveready Batteries in *Drum* magazine, April 1958. Source: Killie Campbell Library, Durban.

Figure 12. Advertisement for Eveready Batteries in *Drum* magazine, October 1958. Source: Killie Campbell Library, Durban.

black hand shines a cone of light on the man's face with a flashlight. The text cautions: "Be safe in the streets tonight! There is no need to be afraid in the night if you carry a torch. Evildoers depend on darkness to do their work—but light scares them away. The friendly light of a torch gives you confidence—lets you see danger before it has a chance to strike. Buy a torch today. Always carry it with you at night—and remember to keep it filled with EVEREADY batteries."[11] The second picture shows a young black man looking through a hole of shattered glass. His eyes look angry, and a bit frightened. His hand reaches out, possibly to grab something or to hold somebody back. Here again, the light of the flashlight from the bottom corner illuminates the face of the evildoer. His deeds do not go unnoticed. The text reads:

> Be safe after dark. Darkness is a time of danger—but you will have no need to fear sudden, unexpected attacks and accidents in the street at night if you carry a torch. The light from the torch gives you the use of your eyes—even in pitch blackness—and lets you see what's coming in time to get out of the way. Whenever you have to go out into the dark take a torch with you—and be safe.[12]

Although the radio campaign and the advertisement in *Drum* magazine come from different political contexts (postapartheid vs. apartheid), both place the responsibility for "being safe" in the hands of the individual, who must deal with the structural failure. During apartheid, the pitch darkness of the township appeared impossible to overcome (neither the development of necessary infrastructure nor the abolishment of apartheid were realistic short-term solutions), but people could move more safely through the night by using Eveready flashlights and batteries, at least per the rationale of the ad. In the same vein, while crime in contemporary South Africa seems insurmountable, people are encouraged to circumvent a hijacking by tuning to the radio or checking an interactive map.

The campaigns from both eras construct a logical link between knowing/seeing and "avoiding" crime/"being safe," but they suggest a difference in how security as self-care is handled. The flashlight is personal, whereas the information regime of instant space depends on communication. In contrast to a cell phone, blog, or mapping tool, a flashlight cannot transmit detailed, unambiguous warnings or crucial information to other people. In addition, the flashlight does not lend itself to planning ahead of time: the piece of information (in the form of an evildoer) shows up directly in front of you, and this is when the flashlight carrier needs to act immediately.

A new regime of security as self-government has emerged that differs from older self-help techniques. My analysis builds on different citizen-run anticrime initiatives in which the police do not play the central role. I especially draw on the work of SA CAN (South African Community Action Network), a crime prevention hub in the Durban suburb of Hillcrest that seeks to facilitate a quick and efficient response to and prevention of crime by involving the residents of the neighborhood in a sophisticated communicative structure. SA CAN calls itself a "patriotic business with attainable vision and strategy for a crime-free, safer South Africa" merging this business with ideals of family-like ties and mutual aid.[13] I connect the story of SA CAN to other initiatives such as the crime bulletin on Durban's radio channel EastCoastRadio, the self-help guide *Safe, Secure, and Streetwise*, as well as various posters and other scraps of urban wallpaper. My analysis builds on initiatives of different spatialities in the city: some, like SA CAN's work in the suburb of Hillcrest, are more spatially bound; others, like radio messages or booklets, are more dispersed spatialities. By following projects of such different spatial foci, I want to probe instant space as a widespread logic reaching beyond one particular place and beyond one particular medium of communication.

My argument builds on visions and strategies expressed by the drivers of these initiatives as laid out in interviews, newsletters, websites, and advertising materials. It is not the purpose of this chapter to ask how successful these initiatives are (neither in terms of outreach nor actual crime prevention). Rather, I am more fascinated with the political vision they follow and what their presence on the urban message board means for "rethinking the urban social" and security as a public good.[14] As urban texts—in trains, in public buildings, on the radio, or on the Web— these initiatives define the problem of violent crime in South Africa in a particular way and suggest solutions of a particular kind. They reflect and shape the contours of the sayable and practicable.[15]

I begin by conceptualizing an idealized citizen figure that I call, following the narratives of my interview partners, *everyone,* and analyze how this self-governing subject becomes the key protagonist in the regime of instant space. Next, I identify three mechanisms centrally involved in governing security as *doing instant space.* These mechanisms are, first, navigation through insecurity; second, the individualization of spaces of security; and third, crime avoidance as survive-style. Later, I shift my focus to the large group of "others" who cannot or do not want to (fully) embrace these new forms of communication, organization, and responsibility: the *no-airtimers* (domestic employees) and the *instant mercenaries* (car guards). Their activation for instant crime prevention by private initiatives and the police reveals the fact that the category of *everyone* is less inclusive than its proponents argue. Finally, I reflect on instant space for a wider theorizing of urban security governance and the consequences of a life in bubbles. How can we rethink fragmentation and governance if urban residents are permanently switched on security seekers?

Everyone

Instant space engenders a "new game of citizenship" whose protagonists I call, following the narratives of my interview partners, *"everyones."*[16] *"Everyone* . . . whether they're a millionaire in his mansion or the hobo on the side of the street," who sees something suspicious should call the free SA CAN emergency line, explains the Duty Manager in the SA CAN Community Intelligence Center. If the information qualifies as important, "we let *everyone* know about it,"[17] which means that the office sends out a text message via computer to (a segment or all of) the then thirty-four thousand subscribed members in the community. The unit of interest for SA CAN is a community of *everyones* who are empowered to act against crime through detailed and immediate information.

No lay people exist in the regime of instant space: in fact, my interview partners frame the activity of *everyones* in the police language of a Weberian state: "The police force is the public themselves," the founder of the SA CAN Community Centre reasons.[18] He begins his thought with the (once central) protagonists of policing, "the police," indeed the police *"force,"* and ends with "the public." Policing, accordingly, is not the job of the police, but is fulfilled by a broader public. He continues: "Everybody is a bobby on the beat, but armed with . . . not [a] firearm:

armed with a cell phone," the SA CAN founder continues.[19] If members of the police have firearms, and if *everyone* is also the police, then *everyone* is armed. But everyone's arms are of a different nature: When an everyone witnesses a crime or something suspicious, he or she is asked to immediately inform the SA CAN office, and through that, the community. "Fire with your phone"[20] could indeed be the slogan for such technologies of postpolice policing.[21] In this sense, the cell phone also becomes an intelligence beacon. By receiving a warning via text message, every person equipped with a cell phone can take precautions to protect herself and avoid a certain area or be on alert about a particular car or person.

The underlying logic of the arms metaphor is that information leads to the avoidance of crime or self-defense. The host of EastCoastRadio Crime Bulletin makes a similar conceptual link between information and arming oneself against crime": "Being forewarned is forearmed. So you know, being warned ahead of time, so it helps you to arm yourself. Not in arm yourself as in a call to arms. . . . So they would often phone us and say 'Where is stuff happening? Which are the hijacking hotspots?'"[22] The arms metaphor is a key element in the theory of change underpinning the regime of instant space: According to the rationale, detailed and up-to-date information about crime helps people make informed choices ("arm themselves") and therefore keep away from the crime.

Anticrime initiatives from EastCoastRadio to SA CAN only address the first step in this causal chain of receiving information to avoiding crime. Although they help the *everyones* to collect, organize, and process the information, and they facilitate an easy "intake," the next steps— whether the person has a choice to act differently and the amount of success that choice brings—are not interfered with. For example, a man on his way to work can be aware of a smash-and-grab-hotspot, yet very likely will not have the choice of taking a different route. The "homines prudentes" of instant space get help to do the survival math, but they must then survive on their own.[23]

DOING INSTANT SPACE

But the constant reference to figures of state police and defense forces is both an exaggeration and an understatement: It not only exaggerates *everyones'* roles in crime fighting (e.g., they do not have the right to arrest a criminal, or shoot someone) but more importantly, it underestimates how deeply security has become entrenched in all spheres of *everyones'* everyday life. Understanding the contemporary and future role for ordinary urbanites in the governance of their own security needs a fresh vocabulary that reaches beyond the reference points of the Weberian state. I suggest it must begin with tracing the contours of *doing instant space*. Doing space, as I have explained earlier, implies a thinking of space as performative—as the multiple productions of urban space and the effects of space on urban subjects. I will characterize *doing instant space* through three mechanisms: navigating through insecurity, individualizing spaces of security, and engaging in survive-style.

Navigating through Insecurity

Instant space is the art of navigating through the city as safely as possible for as long as possible. In contrast to handsome space, the strategies of instant space do not seek to create safer places, but rather, they help people to know more about unsafe places at a particular time and to sharpen their sensors as they move around the city. A poster in a Cape Townian local train advised its passengers: "Be safe. If a coach is empty, go to one that's fuller" (Figure 13).[24]

The poster thematizes insecurity as a structural problem whose solution is placed into the hands of the individual. He or she is asked to look around and decide with best reasoning and intuition whether to stay or to change coaches. Stepping into an empty coach (and worse: staying in it while having realized its emptiness) is irresponsible and potentially unsafe. The poster suggests an approach to security as only existent in temporally and spatially limited situations, situations that have to be constantly renewed and realigned. No situation is stable in time and space; it can tip at any moment, and it can look different just a few meters further or some minutes later. These flickering spatio-temporal perceptions of danger in the present regime of instant space engender an unprecedented requirement to sense and to instantly react. Instant space thus exceeds the general advice of the self-help literature. Up-to-date news on crime has brought about a new quality to the responsibilization of the everyday: news is used like a route planner—not for traffic but for crime.

There have been many attempts over the past years to turn crime mapping—a criminological technique that visualizes the occurrence of crime—into a tool for everyone's use. Though none have been fully

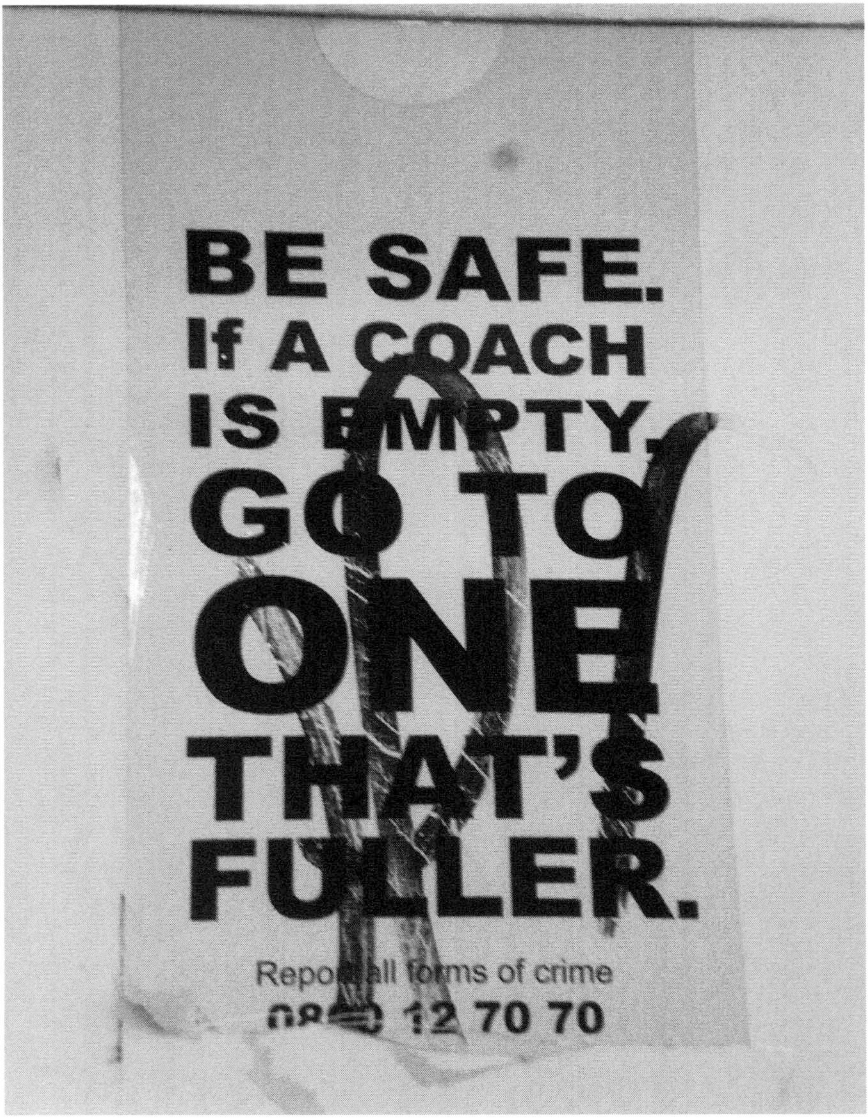

Figure 13. Warning in local trains in Cape Town. Photograph by the author, 2009.

realized in Durban, the mere idea of crime maps and implementing them into everyday crime prevention has sparked great enthusiasm amongst the potential hosts of those phantom interactive maps. East-CoastRadio, for example, planned to install an interactive crime information map where listeners could subscribe as members of a particular neighborhood and enter warnings or crime incidents directly, not only informing others, but being informed by those others as well. New robbery, theft, or hijacking trends were to be generated and posted on the map through the entries of the users. According to the crime bulletin reporter of EastCoastRadio, this is what would make people interested in checking the interactive maps: "[They say]: 'Oh, yes, there are smash and grabs happening around here' or: 'there is my route, I am plotting my route from home to work, so I know what's taken place yesterday along this road. . . .' For example, if you log in and say: 'it happened here in Durban instantly it goes onto this map, the red dots that's there.'"[25]

Crime mapping as a participatory tool allows people to be a part of a bottom-up intelligence production and to create their own risk analysis before they go out into the world. With fresh crime information in the form of a diagram or a map with red stars, people can "do the math" themselves when preparing their movements through the city. A municipal crime mapper enthuses:

> So, straight away, anybody who has access to that information can develop their own kind of analysis or any other role players in industry can say "I am two kilometers from the last hit, it's getting closer to me" and if they have access to it, maybe there is a general intelligence report that says the next strike will be within the next 21 days. If you're within two kilometers of that, it doesn't take a rocket scientist to work out that, "well, in the next 21 days I might be next. In the next 21 days I need to up my game, it's not forever. I maybe only have to hire more security over the next 21 days." And maybe not even for the next 21 days, only on Fridays and Saturdays over the next 21 days.[26]

According to this perception, crime mapping becomes a rational "decision support system" for *everybody,* enabling people to "make the correct decisions based on mathematical systems."[27] They are required to constantly draw the lines between past occurrences and possible future incidents—in a spatially and temporally focused way. In this sense, according to a crime mapping analyst, crime mapping rationalizes people's otherwise often panic-driven judgments.

> [They say] "Look . . . , this is where armed robberies are happening. These are the general times that they are happening. They're targeting people that keep money in the shop, that don't have burglar bars on the windows and stuff like that." I believe people will look at that and then say "Okay, if I need to go to that area, I need to go. [But] A, I need to be more careful [and] B, I need to go outside of these times, because I will have probably less chances of being a victim of crime."[28]

The particular logic of crime mapping and analysis allows for a problem of violent crime to be placed within a temporal and spatial form. A crime problem can now be conceived of as "two hours long in time . . . and . . . five hundred square meters wide,"[29] as the municipal crime mapping analyst reflects. Crime mapping comes with an implied claim to truth and infallibility. As an official in the Department for Community Safety put it: "GIS allows you to map and therefore see. . . . Sometimes you need to see."[30] Seeing becomes a synonym for understanding the truth, and the perfection of the image makes people not only accept and memorize this truth more easily, but also engage within its requirements. Engaging with the knowledge of mapping is the ability to navigate around supposed hotspots, both in space and time. Navigating through insecurity takes the nature of crime as a given; it is a spatial practice focusing on smart movement and surface exploration on the basis of knowledge that needs to be updated constantly in order to react in an appropriate and instantaneous way. Doing instant space for the sake of security is thus a mobile spatial practice, seeking to sharpen the skills of avoidance.

The obsession with space-specific information about crime in instant space is performative: Techniques of instant crime prevention not only transmit the information that a particular place in time is unsafe, but they also mark and materialize it as such.[31] As John and Jean Comaroff point out: "They delineate where order ends and where disorder prevails"[32]—

just in a more nervous way, since distinctions between a safe and an unsafe area are subject to constant adjustment.

Individualizing Spaces of Security

Doing instant space is an individual undertaking. Even if a crime hot-spot visualized on a website is available to everybody who visits it, and even if the same text message is sent out to a large group of people at the same time, *everyone* engages in his own fight against crime.

Dealing with insecurity in an individualized manner is institutional-ized through different insurance-like offers fabricated for individual needs and tastes. SA CAN offers a broad range of anticrime packages for sale. Depending on the respective "top-ups," an "SA CAN family package," an "SOS package" or a "business package" provides paying members with SMS-alert and panic buttons on their cell phones, and with proper crime-scene management. A note at the bottom of the SOS package ad on the website assures the client that the service is worth the money: "In South Africa Today, can you afford to be without this service?"[33] The customizable security packages divide the community of *everyones* into segments according to their varying budgets, preferences, and needs. Packaged like this, security is not a right, or a public good. Instead, the *contrat social* is broken down into an insurance-like arrangement that can be adapted according to individual habits and needs. Security is ren-dered as a question of personal need and taste; any economic possibili-ties or class backgrounds shaping such habits are not mentioned.

The mobile phone as a crime messenger is itself an example of how security governance becomes a personal affair. Crime information liter-ally occurs in people's bags or pockets, next to evening arrangements and love messages. The "urban sensorium" operates from people's pockets: small and powerful.[34] At the same time, in instant space, the cell phone buzzing is no longer a personal affair. It is a citizen's call to duty; therefore, postponing reading the message is irresponsible and can lead to harm.

But there is another crucial dimension: "SA CAN family members" can turn their phones into "a nationwide panic button." "Using cell phone tracking technology, individuals can be tracked once the alarm is activated."[35] In the case of an emergency, SA CAN will then "motivate the relevant policing service providers to your position" and make sure medi-cal assistance is provided. Voluntarily allowing oneself to be traceable as a means of securing personal safety indicates a marked shift in what it means to "watch" people for security reasons. Through enabling an organization to locate a person at every place on the planet that has GPS and cell coverage, *everyones* are not observed or watched (as potential offenders), but are assisted (as potential victims). Being traceable in the regime of instant space is a privilege.[36]

The reality of the panic button gives a particularly clear understanding of how we can imagine instant space as mobile and as opening up around a person's habits and whereabouts. Triggering a panic button wherever a person is creates mobile microspaces of crime prevention. Bubbles of governance thus need to be reconsidered as "specific spaces of immediate action"—personalized and mobile.[37] They surround a person heading home from work or going to the cinema. Of course, the problem with the bubble is that it can burst at any time, because the security protection it offers is often less robust then individuals would like it to be. And even if the bubble is robust, one's neighbor or fellow commuter might have a stronger, less penetrable bubble. This, indeed, is a dimension of the individualization of security spaces that is not mentioned in the discourse about optimizing one's own spaces of security: Everybody is in competition with everybody else for the best bubble that offers the least attractive target for criminals.

Survive-Style

With the cell phone in one's pocket, the safe route downloaded, and the personal security package contracted, crime avoidance becomes a way of life. It is "always with you," the SA CAN website reassures its users. Scrolling down, one can read: "Thank you for visiting the site and have a great CRIME FREE DAY."[38] In order to get through the day—crime free—one needs to adopt a set of practices and habits that together form a routine of "doing crime prevention." In fact, "crime prevention, . . . is like wearing a seat belt," the SA CAN duty manager reasons: "*Everybody* wears a seat belt. But no one used to wear a seat belt until . . . road deaths become a problem. So, it's routine, if you do it three or four times in a row, it will become second nature, and crime prevention should be second nature."[39]

The duty manager suggests that crime prevention, like wearing a seat belt, should be "second nature"—a set of habits and automatisms that we do without thinking, yet with regularity and reliability.[40] The crime bulletin reporter at EastCoastRadio illustrates such good habits: "Listeners [have] gotten used to the idea to picking up their . . . cell phones now wherever they are and, if I am seeing something, I am reporting it."[41] The success, so the radio reporter said, is that listeners have established an ethics of constant alertness and a reaction of sharing information as a way of being responsible.

The seat belt, even if it cannot prevent the accident itself from happening, can save lives; crime prevention, once it has become a personal routine, should be able to do the same.[42] The details of the metaphor matter: the fact that a seat belt can only reduce the devastating effects of an accident and not prevent it from happening is notably analogous to security provision as it is understood in the regime of instant space. Instant crime avoidance techniques accept a high crime rate as inevitable and advise people on how to mitigate their risks and losses by following certain routines.

Instant space appeals to potential victims not to become victims and not to behave like victims. In the foreword to the guide *Safe, Secure, and Streetwise* this rationale becomes clear: "Don't be a victim! . . . : You need not become a victim or another crime statistic—if you take the necessary precautions. The key word is avoidance."[43] By not becoming a victim, a person potentially contributes to bringing down the crime statistics. For this purpose, self-help guides advise people on how to escape from murder or rape; companies, and NGOs offer antihijacking classes; tourist agencies distribute safety tips for tourists. The message is clear: to avoid murder, rape, hijacking or other atrocities, one must take on a particular routine that SA CAN calls "lifestyles of crime prevention."[44] Moving through an unknown area, for example, can be dangerous and therefore needs additional safety performance, as *Safe, Secure, and Streetwise* suggests: "Walking tall: this is as much mental or psychological. Show it by walking erect, with your head high and your shoulders straight. Look as if you know where you're going (even if you don't). Walk purposefully, quickly and confidently even though you may be nervous, or afraid."[45] In a similar spirit, a tourist guide addressing visitors to the 2010 Soccer World Cup sets up safety rules for drivers: "If you're driving, lock your bag in the boot, put your seat belt on and lock your doors. Only leave your windows open by about 5 cm. (But an air-conditioned vehicle is best in our climate anyway!)"[46] Security as second nature shapes attitudes in all domains of people's lives; work, leisure, and body shape all become sites of self-governed security. "You are less likely to fall victim to criminals if you are fit and healthy. Your responses are quicker, you are more alert, and you are likely to get away faster," writes the safety guide.[47]

Striving for security in an instant way is a question of lifestyle, or better, *survive-style,* which means, I suggest, not only surviving in the literal sense, but also the art "of making it"—to work, to the rock concert, to Grandma's house for dinner—through the use of smooth routines and smart choices. Survive-style builds on an attitude of fitness and sensual stimulation, in Bauman's sense. The society of consumption "'interpellates" its members (that is, it addresses them, hails, calls out to, appeals to, questions, but also interrupts and 'breaks in upon' them)" as "consumers-by-vocation."[48] In the society of producers and soldiers, obedience to command and conformity, as well as endurance, submission to monotonous routine, and a readiness to postpone gratification were central behavioral patterns to be internalized in order to make them function in the factory and the battlefield.[49] In contrast, "(post-industrial) life organized around consumption is guided by seduction, ever-rising desires, and volatile wishes." This is what Bauman calls fitness: People must be "ever ready," and have the "ability to rise to the opportunity as it comes, to develop new desires made allurements."[50]

Survive-style is thus the attitude of fitness required in the criminologies of the everyday: a curiosity for new information and the latest trends, and the daily fear translated into an adventure that cries for ever-new skills, services, and products on a security market. It is surviving with elegance and taste. Almost by definition, then, instant crime prevention is exhausting and frustrating; its outcome is uncertain. To use Ian Loader's metaphor, it is like running on a security treadmill: "A treadmill is seldom willingly climbed upon, it calls for constant effort, and such effort leaves one standing precisely where one started (only more exhausted)." Running on this treadmill, Loader writes, leads to "self-perpetuating cycles of activity which makes 'security' less a stable condition of well-being and more a state of endless striving."[51] The type of timely information regarding the spatiality of crime drives the regime of instant space and creates such a self-perpetuating cycle. Just as aesthetics in the regime of handsome space became an end in itself and was often decoupled from the causal chain of safety, information in instant space is acquired, distributed, and visualized—while its actual effects are rarely tracked systematically.

EVERYONES AND THEIR OTHERS

The notion of everyone, as outlined in the chapter so far, depicts an ideal citizen: responsible, informed, and technophile. She lives in a social environment that allows her to create powerful nodes of information exchange and mutual assistance, and to adopt a lifestyle of crime prevention. As the SA CAN duty manager enthuses, she is part of a big, extended family: "We see ourselves as a family. We don't have clients; we have partners. . . . Partners in crime prevention, partners in policing, but family members. We wanna look after our neighbors as [if] they were our sister or our brother or mother or father."[52]

Yet, the family of *everyones* has various *others* who are involved in crime fighting but who are activated through different registers: not through responsibility and trust, but through financial incitements, obligations, and even threats. These actors, I argue, are defined through a lack that either lies within their communicative resources or their will, and this alleged deficiency decisively shapes the way they are being utilized in crime prevention. SA CAN, for example, has a program for those who "cannot afford airtime" specifically targeted toward domestic employees, nannies, and gardeners; hence my description of these subjects as *no-airtimers*.[53] On the other hand, car guards (but equally bar owners, sex workers, or informal traders) are often activated (usually by the police) to share their knowledge about specific crimes, especially in "difficult" communities: communities with little cooperation (among each other or with the police) in the field of crime fighting. Police talk to car guards and bar owners all while being aware that they cannot or do not want to entirely trust them, as these actors might be involved in the very crimes the police are trying to stop. This approach brings these subjects close to a mercenary status, and with regard to their supposedly ambiguous and money-driven commitments as crime fighters in the regime of instant space, I brand them *instant mercenaries*. *No-airtimers* and *instant mercenaries* are figures beyond the wishful family-oriented communities that surround the fantasy of *everyones*.

No-Airtimers

Everyones are not always at home. *Everyones* go to work and, for a great deal of their time out, domestic employees come in and work in their homes. SA CAN has discovered that domestic workers are valuable sources of information who should also be involved in the SA CAN initiative. Getting the domestic workers on board is considered important because of their presence in the homes during the day. As the SA CAN manager knows, "pretty much 60 percent of the day, the domestic workers are at the homes. The homeowners are away at work. They know what is going on in the community."[54]

The group of potentially vigilant people is divided, then, into a community of homeowners and a population of temporal watchers of other peoples' homes. SA CAN tried to roll out its model into the "rural" areas, but found people's "different culture" of problem solving, their reservations toward creating similar organizational structures, and their reluctance to acknowledge crime and violence as major problems not exactly suitable to the project. The "rural" communities, which are, in other words, mainly African, in mainly poor areas, do not seem to fit in with the conception of everyone—an interestingly quick judgment from the part of a project that aims to be a model for the whole of South Africa.

It did not take SA CAN long to find ways to reach out to these communities. Since October 2009, the SA CAN family newsletter has also appeared in Zulu. Hillcrest homeowners are asked to print out the Zulu versions of the newsletters and pass the information to the staff to take home. SA CAN in 2009 had 8,200 township and rural community residents who had registered for Township SOS and Workers against Crime trainings and services.[55] Workers against Crime is SA CAN's program for involving domestic workers in their infrastructure of communication. A specification clarifies whom this addresses: "Those who cannot afford airtime." As "all of [the domestic workers] got cell phones, but none of them have airtime . . . to phone," and homeowners do not usually allow them to use their landline, SA CAN has implemented a so-called "please-call-me-system." The manager explains: "We just say to them, 'just send us a "please call me" and we will phone you back.' So there is . . . never a reason for them to say 'there was no ability to phone anyone.'"[56]

This statement assumes that domestic workers not only lack the resources to make an urgent phone call, but that they also lack the will to take responsibility for crime prevention. The fact that "rewards are offered for information leading to positive arrests" shows how much the mobilization of the no-airtime-community differs from that of the community of everyones: not through appeals to rational or responsible individuals, but through remuneration and obligation.[57] Daily crime prevention becomes part of the job description.

This aspect of the SA CAN model shows that in such "new games of citizenship," not every player is addressed as a citizen. The dividing line can be drawn, first, with regard to the assumed, potential involvement in crime: the mobilization of the *no-airtimers* assumes that they, in one way or another, come from the same social community as criminals, while *everyones* are constructed as the criminals' "other." The second line is drawn between civic responsibility and work requirements. The homeowners are lucky enough to align their self-interest (protecting their house and possessions) with their sense of responsibility as neighbors (watching out, letting others know). Structurally, the domestic employees do not have a comparable interest in their boss's house. Hence, their incentive has to be based on something else, such as a financial reward and/or by making cooperation a work obligation. Related to this is a third factor: domestic employees matter as channels through which information passes (or in the words of the SA CAN duty manager, "as passive and aggressive information flow"), not as potential victims or responsible citizens. Their vulnerability does not count to the same degree; they seem "ungrievable."[58]

The fourth dividing line appears in the seemingly minimal question of airtime or no airtime. *No airtime* has to do with a lack of resources to buy airtime on a regular basis, and it has consequences: no airtime means no active use of a cell phone. If phones are the weapons in this new network of governance, no airtime equals no ammunition to make use of the weapons. If a phone is the entry ticket into the world of volunteer crime prevention, then not having airtime means not having full membership in that world, which leads to a reduced benefit for that particular user. The free "please-call-me-message" introduced by SA CAN cannot entirely make up for these different starting positions. In fact, it contributes to marking and remaking the differences, instead of overcoming them.

There cannot effectively be *everyones* as long there are *no-airtimers*. In the theory of instant space, *everyone* can be an *everyone*. In practice, however, somebody's will is not enough, and membership becomes complicated through social positions, access, and resources.

Instant Mercenaries

Just as *everyones* have various others working within the regime of instant space, old-school police also operate with a number of helpers who aren't addressed as "responsible citizens." These instant mercenaries—downtown car guards, bar keepers, sex workers, and street traders—often operate on an informal level and are therefore vulnerable to law enforcement officers on the one hand, and criminals on the other. Car guards are not officially recognized in Durban and operate on the fringes of legality; bar owners rarely have the required license to sell liquor, and their premises are often raided or closed down; traders rarely hold the right permit and are often chased away; and most sex workers operate illegally and are vulnerable to police humiliations. Even though these professional activities are on the periphery of legality, the police and certain municipal initiatives have discovered the benefits of utilizing them as sources of information about past and possible future crime. Their abilities to watch, to gather information, and to supposedly influence others make them a valuable source of instant crime intelligence.

Car guards are informal entrepreneurs who watch parked cars all over the city of Durban. Their earnings are minimal and depend on the generosity of their clients, who, after parking, may provide them with change. Being a car guard is not a formal occupation in Durban; car guards are not armed, and their ability to protect cars is primarily symbolic in nature. Their rootedness in the urban landscape and their daily presence at the same spot make them a convenient source of information. But most importantly, "the car guards know the criminal element," as a commissioner in the organized crime division states.[59] In contrast to the police, they merge and blend in with the downtown urban jungle. Recruiting is easy, as the commissioner describes:

> I can easily approach a car guard, if it's a black car guard I will go behind the corner and make [whistles]. And I will speak to him and say: "Listen, I will give you money . . ." I'll give him money like 20 bucks. Just to

get attention. And then I'll say to him: "Listen, I am giving you money from my pocket now, if you meet with me at the Wimpy, far away from here, . . . and if you give me information about what you saw yet, I am sure you did, I'll get some more money for you."[60]

According to the commissioner's narration of the recruitment process, the beginning of the relationship consists of payment (to "get attention") and the promise of even more payment (in exchange for information). The assumption is that money is the only, or at least the safest, way to involve a car guard in policing relevant information networks. So, in contrast to *everyones*, who are invited to attend the community police forum, send SMSs, or report crime on the radio as a matter of *duty*, car guards are encouraged with money. They are not approached as civic actors who act responsibly in the public sphere, but as marginal entrepreneurs who extend their watching and reporting activities in their place of work, not unlike the domestic workers. They are imagined and treated as mercenary watchers, rather then as watching citizens.

Noncompliance is implicated: "I am sure you saw something" points to the *instant mercenaries* being watched. Car guards are usually suspected of being involved in the theft of vehicles. Like *no-airtimers*, they are expected to be socially close to criminals, at least in having observed them or talked to them, if not having actively worked with them. While the police willingly seek out and hire these individuals, they may still investigate and arrest them, showing a clear awareness of the dual nature of their relationship with these *instant mercenaries*.[61]

One car guard, Joe, who keeps informing the police without being rewarded (despite numerous promises), stated he does not "help the police because of money, but because he wants to be responsible."[62] He clearly constructs himself as a good citizen, which is in contrast to many accounts about car guards by other actors of the municipality or the police. He had been a car guard for nearly ten years when I talked to him, and he saw himself as the agent of law and order in "his" parking lot. He helped uncover a big drug deal at his parking lot, and informs the police when car theft syndicates try to use the parking lot. According to his account, members of the police often get promoted through the information he provides them with. "Sometimes you risk your life for other people's cars and sometimes they don't say thank you. I don't want money from people. Just thank you."[63] He often finds wallets and hands them over to the nearby hotel, commenting: "This is how honest me is."[64] The dominant perception within formal policing organizations is that car guards lack civic responsibility, and their desire for money is the only way to make use of them in crime prevention. This seems, however, to underestimate the actual civil commitment of some of the individuals involved.

The effort to involve car guards in policing is an attempt to build, with a carrot-and-stick approach, a community of place-specific watchers and providers of information who are viewed as solid elements in a fluid downtown area with a lot of fluctuation. Mobilizing such marginal entrepreneurs to watch more than cars entails risks for all involved. Not only is crime watching outsourced from the police to nonpolice, but the dangers that go along with it are outsourced as well: car guards run high risks of being victimized by car thieves, drug dealers, and others who are not pleased with the additional surveillance. At the same time, some car guards offer their watching services to the "other side," such as to car theft syndicates or drug dealers, for a higher fee.[65] State officials do not own, and therefore cannot control, the services of these independent entrepreneurs, so they can never be sure whom to really trust. A mist of mistrust spreads across this regime of instant knowledge provision. By positioning these car guards as mercenaries rather than citizens, the police not only insult those who may be willing to help them but also link their loyalties to financial reward, thereby limiting these relationships to simple exchange relationships.

By constructing domestic employees, gardeners, or car guards as only being motivated by financial rewards and not out of a sense responsibility, both SA CAN and the police participate in creating a two-class activation system in which the notion of *everyone* covers just one idealized and particularistic subject position. Distrust, financial incentives, work obligations, and threats are the driving features through which these marginalized actors are selectively, and sometimes reluctantly, drawn into the crime fighting community. Here, the commercial nature of these "criminologies of the *everyone*" becomes more clearly visible than in the calls to responsibility that the (often also money-based) programs operate with. The *instant mercenaries* and *no-airtimers* are helpers, no more than that; they are not considered *everyone*-citizens, but as a means through which to get direct information. The existence of *no-airtimers* and *instant mercenaries* in the regime of instant space makes the universalism of the *everyones* an illusion.

OUTSMARTING CRIME AND THE INSTANT BUBBLE

Instant space *has* no security. It *is* not safe. Security, in this regime, only exists as a fortunate concatenation of situational experiences—each of which is the result of continuous striving by means of smart routines, communicative alliances, and receptiveness to any piece of potentially life-saving information. By doing the survival math successfully, the subjects of instant space can outsmart crime, as it were, but will never know for how long.

Earlier in this book I argued that we need to rethink the way we conceptualize fragmented cityness and governance. In my conceptualization of handsome space, bubbles of governance appeared to be fixed spaces imbued with a particular affective and aesthetic quality. In instant space, bubbles of governance are mobile, situational, and personal. They envelop a person while she moves through the city, when she reports something suspicious, when she reads a warning message on her cell phone display, or when she "walks tall." If ordinary urban residents govern (their own) security in this way—whoever they are, wherever they are—the spaces of security governance travel with them. And if such splintered security governance is shaped by and further reinforces social and spatial fragmentation, we should also rethink the nature of fragmentation itself as less spatially fixed, more mobile, and made of communicative routines and consumerist choices.

Lieven De Cauter has described our daily life in cities "as a movement via transportation capsules from one enclave or capsule (home for instance) to another (campus, office, airport, all-in hotel, mall, and so on)."[66] Building on De Cauter, Rowland Atkinson has formed the notion of the "flowing enclave." For both authors, the enclave, mobile or not, is a space of exclusivity: "A space which flows and is created by the affluent in ways that aid the management of risk and engagement with social difference in the city. . . . The qualities of the neighborhood as a defensive space are made portable."[67] Like Atkinson's floating enclaves, instant bubbles are mobile and can be imagined as defensible spaces in motion. However, the bubbles of instant crime prevention discussed in this chapter are more permeable and inclusive than theorists of urban dystopias assume. EastCoastRadio's desire to have their crime bulletin reach "everyone," or SA CAN's dream of having "everyone" report criminal incidents immediately, evoke an ideal of a community of crime fighters that connects across different groups and walks of life. The partial and differentiating involvement of groups of "others," however, gives a sense of the limited horizon of such initiatives with universalizing language. Rather than being activated as responsible citizens, these others are activated as helpers or mercenary-type persons, always in the service of someone else, working on behalf of someone else's bubble. The result is an awkwardly fragmented landscape composed of (self-) governance bubbles, made less from the spatial disconnection between the bubbles and their impermeability of imagined safety than from the very complex connectivity and permeability that the bubbles create. Fragmented urban landscapes in postapartheid South Africa must then be rethought through their connectivity and porosity. A blunt diagnosis of a new apartheid, an apartheid based on class, cannot capture the entanglements between emerging mobile, technologized, and communicative modes of social sorting with older, more rigid forms of segregation.

In his work on African cities, AbdouMaliq Simone has conceptualized the innovative and improvisational ways by which people build a sense of stability in the face of a constant uncertainty and volatility of the arrangements of their social existence.[68] With "people as infrastructure," Simone describes the "ability of residents to engage complex combinations of objects, spaces, persons, and practices. These conjunctions become an infrastructure—providing for and reproducing life in the city."[69] Simone has built his concept around marginalized urbanites, who weave such connections in order to get better access to resources such as housing, security, or education. However, the techniques of instant space can be conceptualized as a part of urbanites' attempt to build connections and opportunities when official infrastructures do not function well enough. Instant space is then not reducible to a middle-class urge to disconnect itself from the rest of the city, but is itself a form of social infrastructure that people create when they cannot take a functioning infrastructure of security for granted. Instant space is then not only the phenomenon of responsibilization and governance at a distance, but also a set of everyday practices of survival. The larger question that instant space hints at is how different communities—such as wealthy and poor, by car or on foot, with smartphone or without—build their respective infrastructures of survival and how they implicate one another in their respective infrastructures—as citizens, helpers, mercenaries, or others. Instant space with its taste for excessive information intake and *survive-style* is only one of those infrastructures of cityness that urban studies must yet attend to.

CONCLUSION

Making Love to the City

Writing about a night market in Jakarta, AbdouMaliq Simone reflects on its capacity to surprise: "The best deal, the best story, or the best opportunity will not be found in the place traders and customers expect to find them."[1] To take the city by surprise, as he puts it, means advancing on uncertain terrain, and in doing so, taking risks. Forging ahead across urban unpredictability necessitates figuring out who is who and whom to trust. It opens the space for collective maneuvering, and just maybe in the end, it helps to make things better for an urban majority.

Seeking security seems to be the opposite. The efforts people take to be safe that I have described in this book are to avoid the bad surprise by making it calculable in space and time, by "outcharming" and "outsmarting" it. While the surprises of unexpected offers, better deals, or the new gossip of the night market are surely intriguing, the surprises waiting in a city where crime is as dramatic as in Durban can be devastating. Letting the city take you by surprise in Durban is, simply put, too risky.

The dilemma is profound. It is that of living in an uncertain world and managing it. While the sheer number and violence of the crimes haunting postapartheid South Africa might be unique, insecurity and uncertainty are conditions shared all over the world. Securing physical safety, a place to stay, and a job that pays a living wage have become increasingly difficult, not only in the postcolony, but also in what we call the West, where financial crises, welfare state cutbacks, and austerity politics have made urban lives ever more precarious.

Some scholars thus tell us to look to the South in order to know what's coming in the North or the West. I don't believe that reversing the normative linearism that has dominated social sciences for so long is the way to go. The present and the future of different urbanities is multifaceted, and neither the South African crime crisis, nor the South African way of coming to terms with it will predict or pave the way to urban futures elsewhere.[2] Rather than deducing from Durban what awaits other cities, I am interested in the shared experience that cuts across a world of cities. Thinking about shared urban experiences is to ask what Durban's history of racial segregation and rampant inequality, as well as its residents' sense of physical insecurity and their mistrust in the state, has to do with urban conditions elsewhere. As my thoughts on security and its bubbles come to a close, I want to reflect on some of the tropes that, however particular they may be to Durban, reverberate with urban ("real" as well as theoretical) formations elsewhere.

Seeking Security in Flirting and Fleeing

In Durban, seeking security means that nothing can be left to chance. From security-friendly designs and atmospheric tricks to contracting the right security package or listening to the crime news on the radio, security is not just there to dwell in or to make a claim upon, but must be achieved every day anew. It is a constant striving, a permanent preparation with an uncertain outcome. Security does not "exist" as such, other than in temporarily and spatially defined experiences. While talk about crime is common, and the problem is recognized as systemic, the solutions are placed in the hands of the individual, who is assisted by devices and agencies that all promise instant infallible solutions. Security, far from being a public good, has become the promise to be delivered through much strenuous striving.

This striving, as I have argued throughout the book, is intrinsically spatial. While alarm systems, electric fences, and other "sovereign" manifestations of governing through space are widespread, my concern has been with the softer, affective, and communicative techniques of security, which belong to the double notion of flirting and fleeing. Flirting through space, as I conceptualized in "Handsome Space," aims at making places irresistibly charming and, this is the hope, safe. Fleeing through space, as I laid out in "Instant Space," captures the techniques of urban residents on the go, trying to avoid the worst. Flirting is place-bound, fleeing is mobile, and each depends on the other: Where the flirt doesn't catch on (yet, or anymore, or it's not for you), fleeing becomes ever more critical.

Flirting and fleeing are techniques of communication, though different in their appeal. Flirting relies on the idea that places "speak," or indeed, whisper into your ear, and that a good manager of a bar, a business improvement district, or a parking lot can involve all sorts of actants into such charm talks, from music to wall decoration, from functioning garbage collection to convincing dress codes. The hope is to lure in the good denizens and to discretely but infallibly let them know what the rules of the place are. More explicit communication, it seems, is the last resort—offered only when the more implicit messages are not effective. Fleeing, on the other hand, needs instant and explicit verbal and visual communication about the wheres and whens of crime. The panic button, the interactive maps, the call-in systems, and the countless behavioral tricks for avoiding muggings, robberies, or hijackings are all instances of these communicative efforts and of a shared belief in the causal chain of movement from "knowing" to "avoiding."

Flirting and fleeing are rationalities of government that stretch beyond security. One does not need much fantasy to discover the logic of flirting in all sorts of official charm offensives, from city branding and other urban love-marketing to competitive hyper-building or organized gentrification. Here, flirting is dazzling, making surfaces the measure of everything. Fleeing, too, is a pervasive logic of governing, or of refusing to do so, when municipalities disengage from their responsibility to provide affordable housing, education, health, or transport for all. Decades of privatizing and outsourcing public services in cities around the globe tell a story of withdrawal and of giving up on the idea that cities, in their entirety, can be provided with necessary infrastructure and social goods. As logics of government, then, flirting and fleeing are frustrating: they are superficial, impatient, and fragmentative; they are obsessed with the here and now, and are reluctant to address social problems in their historical and political depth.

But there is potential yet in the notions of flirting and fleeing when we do not solely understand them as logics of governance but as ways of being in the city. Flirting involves playing, making a move without showing one's cards. It might be promiscuous whenever it promises too much to too many people, playing too incautiously with too many feelings, or expectations. It often treads close to a lie, yet what fascinates me about flirting is that it posits a (however preliminary, however half-true) "yes," an affirmation that includes the stranger and the projects whose shapes are less than clear.

If flirting enacts the (however ambiguous) "yes," then fleeing practices a "no"—that is, in temporarily disappearing, but also in trespassing, or refusing to be sorted in a particular way. Fleeing is cityness as a kind of escape, a practice, perhaps a fate, shared. While flirting comes with a grain of utopian urbanism in reaching out to the other, fleeing takes us to the dystopian city where everybody is on the run. To be sure, the motivations and conditions for this fleeing differ significantly depending on whether you make your way to the office from the township or the townhouse, whether you are a homeless teenager or an undocumented worker from Mozambique, whether you are a woman or a man, black or white. Some navigate with a panic button and the "safe" route on their smart phones; others do without airtime or membership in the relevant networks. As everyday practices, flirting and fleeing are never *just* about what people do to be safe, but lead us directly to the conditions that bring those practices about and transform the norms of what it takes to be safe in the city.

DEFAMILIARIZATION

With flirting and fleeing, the categories of private and public, of privileged and precarious, of citizenship and survival, and of governing and (not) being governed cannot be taken for granted. Perhaps the ensuing ambiguities make flirting and fleeing well suited for the project of defamiliarization that postcolonial scholars believe to be key for creating a more cosmopolitan urban studies.[3] In the cosmopolitan awakening of urban studies over the past decade, much attention has been paid to the need to de-center "geographical reference points" in urban scholarship by "writing the world" from places formerly off the map and not allowing New York, London, or Berlin to define what counts as urban, global, and theory relevant.[4]

But decentering is not enough—one can engage in cosmopolitan urbanism from Paris or be stuck in Western universalism when writing from Lagos. The exciting exercise begins *after* we have agreed on the claim that theory comes from everywhere.[5] It might start with taking the risk of letting go of epistemological certainties and instead making puzzlement and "negative epiphanies" our points of engagement.[6] In the end, cities, in Africa and elsewhere, might still remain "unknowable" or "leaking"—indeed "fleeing" from our attempts to make sense of them.[7]

But perhaps cities are only fleeing from the too-fixed ascriptions of themselves. More than attempting to provide a set of answers, *Security in the Bubble* has offered a way of *asking* a modest yet curious "how": how security is sought in and through space, and how this departs from earlier ways of governing through space in South Africa, and how it reverberates with broader political techniques in cities elsewhere. Handsome and instant space are only two possible ways of telling the story of the spatial life of security in postapartheid Durban. They are certainly not offering an exhaustive truth about peoples' longing for a safe life, but they have allowed me to address two dimensions that have so far been eluded in most postapartheid urban analyses.

SURVIVALZENSHIP

If the many acts of watching out for oneself, one's neighbor, or one's place are at the core of a new kind of (urban) citizenship in postapartheid South Africa, as some of the protagonists in this book have claimed, how can we come to terms with it? Citizenship, to be sure, is not meant here as a formal status or membership, but as collective acts of responsibility and as a relation between rights and obligations. Perhaps, *survivalzenship* is the most appropriate term to describe the kind of citizenship whose acts of engagement consist of surviving, in the broadest and in the narrowest terms, and ideally, with intelligence and finesse. It is the art of making it; it stretches into all spheres of life, from gardening to "walking tall," and it takes for granted an ability to make this striving a priority in one's daily life. Yet, however all encompassing these practices aiming at security are, as acts of (urban) citizenship they disappoint.[8] The survivalzenship of handsome and instant space stretches over the city and urban lives, but it is strikingly narrow: stuck in the bubble of imagined safety, divided within it, and cultivating a kind of urban user-literacy.

First, in handsome and instant space, one is not a citizen of the city, but a denizen of a place in time, a downtown club, a townhouse complex, a network of users, or a community of radio listeners. The bubble is not the *city in an essence*, but in many cases it forms itself against the city, seeking to be different, exceptional. The language of "priority zones," "corridors of excellence," and "improvement precincts" mirrors this spirit of distinction. Seeing like a bubble, therefore, is not seeing like a small city.[9] If the city is a marketplace of unpredictability, the bubble must stick out from the city. Rather than taking the city itself as its substance for engagement, "survivalzenship" is thus about surviving despite and against the city.

Second, even within the bubbles, citizenship is not for everyone. Those at the fringes of handsome space who must be reminded that the place is not for sleeping or for defecating, are not citizens of the bubble. And the car guards and gardeners who are drawn into instant space through financial awards, work obligation, or threats are not made responsible as citizens either, but as helpers in the name of security. Even as many safety initiatives assume that "everyone" is, or can be, part of the crime-fighting community, survivalzenship is a subjectivity of different sorts. Passing, dwelling, moving, flirting, or fleeing happen differently according to who you are in terms of race and class position.

Third, if living in the city means learning and becoming literate,[10] the kind of urban literacy acquired in seeking security is a user literacy. Being a citizen involves some ability to rewrite the rules of the game,[11] but the skills that handsome and instant space require and reward are not for rewriting the rules of the game or even for grasping the game. The techniques that handsome and instant space offer and facilitate are not about understanding the political, social, and historical dimensions of the ongoing security crisis but are obsessed with here-and-now solutions. The "everyones" on their way to circumvent the hotspots of crime are avoiding the blind spots of postapartheid politics. Survivalzenship is thus a kind of citizenship that is dramatically alienated from the political. The survivalzenship practiced in the many safety initiatives in South Africa is an urgent here-and-now commitment that is disengaged from a longue durée of black dispossession and racial brutality in South Africa and from the continuing social injustice in the present.

MAKING LOVE TO THE CITY

If the bubble frustrates us due to the limits it poses on solidarity and citizenship, what is the way out of it? I believe that it begins with thinking of the city, not the bubble, as a space of mutuality. This means to take the city, not the bubble, as a space of learning. To learn, according to McFarlane, is not always strategic, not often linear, but incremental.[12] Learning the city happens in assemblage; it must do with what's there, including the "ruins" of older urban regimes and the people whose walks of life one cannot identify with.[13] Becoming literate in and of the city is not always nice, never safe, but messy and uncertain. It is about collective trials and errors, about having some "faith in the city" even when the city doesn't seem to inspire much hope.[14]

The task, then, is to take back the flirt and the charm offensive from "lovemark capitalism" and the surface politics that have come to dominate our cities. To flirt is, according to an older usage, to make love (even if the intentions are not always straightforward or "for real").[15] Making love to the city can mean many things. But I want to inscribe it into a "politics of care," a cultivation of a shared "affective commons,"[16] where spaces of empathy are stretched to involve those who are not cousins or neighbors. This "commensality," as Mbembe calls it,[17] needs an urban politics courageous enough to see the city in its entirety and to embed the striving for security into the much larger project of ensuring capabilities for the majority.

Elements of infrastructure are critical for such a project of making love to the city, because they determine what can flow from where to where, who gets connected and who is cut off, how public resources are allocated through water pipes, roads, and trains. They lay out paths through which urbanites do or do not come together,[18] and they condition what people can, and think they can, do with one another in the city. Infrastructure "attracts people, draws them in, coalesces and expends their capacities."[19] As lying "beneath the social,"[20] infrastructure has a different depth and durée than the surface spatiality of handsome and instant space. And perhaps this depth, together with its purpose to connect, makes it the real litmus test for postapartheid spatial transformation. Making love to the city must hence be understood in such political, infrastructural ways: as an enabling act that allows for a conviviality that the landscape of bubbles does not offer. Creating infrastructures with the urban majority in mind can be a real "engagement" to the city and might conjure a safer place for all. The hope is that in the end, then, South Africa could become "the speech-act of a certain way of being in common rather than side by side."[21]

Notes

Introduction

1. Teresa P. R. Caldeira, *City of Walls: Crime, Segregation, and Citizenship in Sao Paulo* (Berkeley: University of California Press, 2000); Mike Davis, "Planet of Slums: Urban Involution and the Informal Proletariat," *New Left Review* 26 (2004): 5–34; Oren Yiftachel, "Critical Theory and 'Gray Space': Mobilization of the Colonized," *CITY* 13, no. 2 (2009): 247–63; Slavoj Žižek, "How to Begin: From the Beginning," *New Left Review* 57 (2009); George Galster, *Driving Detroit: The Quest for Respect in the Motor City* (Philadelphia: University of Pennsylvania Press, 2012); Martin Murray, "The Spatial Dynamics of Postmodern Urbanism: Social Polarisation and Fragmentation in Sao Paulo and Johannesburg," *Journal of Contemporary African Studies* 22, no. 2 (2004): 139–64.

2. Nancy Fraser, "From Discipline to Flexibilization? Rereading Foucault in the Shadow of Globalization," *Constellations* 10, no. 2 (2003): 160–71.

3. Martin Murray, *Taming the Disorderly City: The Spatial Landscape of Johannesburg after Apartheid* (Ithaca: Cornell University Press, 2008), 35.

4. Patrick Bond, "South Africa's Frustrating Decade of Freedom: From Racial to Class Apartheid," *Monthly Review* 55, no. 10 (2004): 45–59.

5. Clifford Shearing and Jennifer Wood introduced the term "bubble of governance" to describe different sorts of "communal spaces, such as shopping malls or Business Improvement Districts, in which usually more affluent people are able to extend service provision. These bubbles are often not accessible to poorer people, whose limited abilities of consumption disqualify them from the status of "denizen" in these areas; they are often "left to live and work in spaces surrounding the bubbles." See Clifford Shearing and Jennifer Wood, "Nodal Governance, Denizenship and Communal Space: Challenges to the Westphalian Ideal," in *Limits to Liberation after Apartheid: Citizenship, Governance*

and Culture, ed. Steven Robins (Oxford: James Currey, 2005), 105; George S. Rigakos and David R. Greener, "Bubbles of Governance: Private Policing and the Law in Canada," *Canadian Journal of Law and Society* 15, no. 1 (2000): 145–86.

6. Chronotopes, as borrowed from the Russian cultural theorist Mikhail Bakhtin, are space-times or time-specific spatialities. See Mikhail Bakhtin, "Forms of Time and the Chronotope of the Novel," in *The Dialogic Imagination*, ed. Mikhail Bakhtin (Austin: University of Texas Press, 1981). For an ingenious adoption of Bakhtin's concept to the analysis of governance see Mariana Valverde, *Chronotopes of Law: Jurisdiction, Scale, and Governance* (London: Routledge, 2015); Mariana Valverde, *Law and Order: Images, Meanings, Myths* (New Brunswick: Rutgers University Press, 2006); Dawn Moore and Mariana Valverde, "Maidens at Risk: 'Date Rape Drugs' and the Formation of Hybrid Risk Knowledges," *Economy and Society* 29, no. 4 (2000): 514–31.

7. This kind of handsome spatial governance, to be sure, always goes hand in hand with "harder" forms of policing and spatial management. My endeavor is to offer a change in perspective, namely to see aesthetic and affective means of spatial governmentality not as the little sister of broken-windows style policing, as it were, but as a logic in its own right.

8. David Crouch, *Flirting with Space* (London: Ashgate, 2010), 1.

9. Sarah Nuttall, *Entanglement: Literary and Cultural Reflections on Post-Apartheid* (Johannesburg: Wits University Press, 2009), 151.

10. Achille Mbembe, "Necropolitics," *Public Culture* 15, no. 1 (2003): 39.

11. Nuttall, *Entanglement*, 151–52.

12. AbdouMaliq Simone, "The Right to the City," *Interventions* 7, no. 3 (2005): 323.

13. Edgar Pieterse, "Building with Ruins and Dreams: Some Thoughts on Realising Integrated Urban Development in South Africa through Crisis," *Urban Studies*, 43, no. 2 (2006): 285–304.

14. Charles Landry, *The Art of City-Making* (London: Earthscan, 2007), 39.

15. Richard Florida, *Who's Your City? How the Creative Economy Is Making Where to Live the Most Important Decision of Your Life* (New York: Basic Books, 2008).

16. By cityness AbdouMaliq Simone means "the city as a thing in the making . . . the common sense of our urban experience." See AbdouMaliq Simone, *City Life from Jakarta to Dakar: Movements at the Crossroads* (London: Routledge, 2010), 3, 4; see also Edgar Pieterse, "Grasping the Unknowable: Coming to Grips with African Urbanisms," *Social Dynamics* 37, no. 1 (2011): 5–23.

17. Nigel Thrift, "Intensities of Feeling: towards a Spatial Politics of Affect," *Geografiska Annaler* 86, no. 1 (2004): 57–78.

18. Martina Löw, *Soziologie der Städte* (Frankfurt am Main: Suhrkamp, 2008), 76; Fiona Ross, "Sense-Scapes: Senses and Emotion in the Making of

Place," lecture given at the University of Cape Town, October, 7, 2009; Karen Rodriguez, *Small City on a Big Couch: A Psychoanalysis of a Provincial Mexican City* (New York: Rodopi, 2012).

19. Oscar Newman, *Defensible Space: Crime Prevention through Urban Design* (London: Macmillan, 1972); James Q. Wilson and George L. Kelling, "Broken Windows," *Atlantic*, March 1982, 1–16; C. Ray Jeffery, *Crime Prevention through Environmental Design* (Beverly Hills, Calif.: Sage, 1971); Ronald V. Clarke, *Situational Crime Prevention: Successful Case Studies* (Albany, N.Y.: Harrow and Heston, 1992).

20. Markus Felson, *Crime and Everyday Life* (Thousand Oaks, Calif.: Pine Forge Press, 1998), 164.

21. Critically: David Garland, "The New Criminologies of Everyday Life: Routine Activity Theory in Historical and Social Context," in *Ethical and Social Perspectives on Situational Crime Prevention*, ed. Andrew von Hirsch, David Garland, and Alison Wakefield (Oxford: Hart Publishing, 2000), 221; Adam Crawford, "Situational Crime Prevention, Urban Governance and Trust Relations," in *Ethical and Social Perspectives on Situational Crime Prevention*, ed. Andrew von Hirsch, David Garland, and Alison Wakefield (Oxford: Hart Publishing, 2000), 194; Malcolm Feeley and Jonathan Simon, "The New Penology: Notes on the Emerging Strategy of Corrections and Its Implications," *Criminology* 30, no. 4 (1992): 449–74.

22. David Garland, *The Culture of Control: Crime and Social Order in Contemporary Society* (Chicago: University of Chicago Press, 2001), 171.

23. Clarke, *Situational Crime Prevention*, 92; Ronald V. Clarke and John Eck, *Become a Problem-Solving Crime Analyst in 55 Small Steps* (London: Jill Dando Institute of Crime Science, UCL London, 2003).

24. Steve Herbert and Elizabeth Brown, "Conceptions of Space and Crime in the Punitive Neoliberal City," *Antipode* 38, no. 4 (2006): 755–77; Sally Engle Merry, *Urban Danger: Life in a Neighborhood of Strangers* (Philadelphia: Temple University Press, 1981).

25. Herbert and Brown, "Conceptions of Space and Crime," 758; Patrick F. Parnaby, "Crime Prevention through Environmental Design: Discourses of Risk, Social Control, and a Neo-liberal Context," *Canadian Journal of Criminology and Criminal Justice*, 48, no. 1 (2006): 9; Laura J. Huey and Richard V. Ericson, "Policing Fantasy City," in *Re-Imagining Policing in Canada*, ed. Dennis Cooley (Toronto: University of Toronto Press, 2005), 148; Ash Amin, "Rethinking the Urban Social," *City* 11, no. 1 (2007): 105.

26. Bernard E. Harcourt, *Illusion of Order: The False Promise of Broken Windows Policing* (Cambridge, Mass.: Harvard University Press, 2001); Bernd Belina, *Raum, Überwachung, Kontrolle: Vom Staatlichen Zugriff auf Städtische Bevölkerung* (Münster: Westfälisches Dampfboot, 2006), 122 ff; Gary T. Marx,

"What's New about the 'New Surveillance'? Classifying for Change and Continuity," *Surveillance and Society* 1, no. 1 (2002): 9–29; Susanne Krasmann, *Die Kriminalität der Gesellschaft: Zur Gouvernementalität der Gegenwart* (Konstanz: UVK, 2003).

27. Jock Young, *The Exclusive Society* (London: Sage, 1999), 130.

28. Jennifer Robinson, *Ordinary Cities: Between Modernity and Development* (London: Routledge, 2006), 2.

29. Jean Comaroff and John L. Comaroff, *Theory from the South: Or, How Euro-America Is Evolving toward Africa* (Boulder, Colo.: Paradigm Publishers, 2011); Raewyn Connell, *Southern Theory: Social Science and the Global Dynamics of Knowledge* (Cambridge, Mass.: Polity Press, 2007).

30. Comaroff and Comaroff, *Theory from the South*, 1.

31. Achille Mbembe and Sarah Nuttall, "Writing the World from an African Metropolis," *Public Culture* 16, no. 3 (2004): 347–72; Achille Mbembe, *On the Postcolony* (Berkeley: University of California Press, 2001); John L. Comaroff and Jean Comaroff, "Law and Disorder in the Postcolony: An Introduction," in *Law and Disorder in the Postcolony*, ed. Jean Comaroff and John L. Comaroff, 1–56 (Chicago: University of Chicago Press, 2006).

32. Connell, *Southern Theory*, ix; see also: Ackbar Abbas, "Faking Globalization," in *Other Cities, Other Worlds*, ed. Andreas Huyssen (Durham: Duke University Press, 2008); Jennifer Robinson, "Global and World Cities: A View from off the Map," *International Journal of Urban and Regional Research* 26, no. 3 (2002): 531–54; Ananya Roy, "The 21st Century Metropolis: New Geographies of Theory," *Regional Studies* 43, no. 6 (2009): 818–30.

33. Robinson, *Ordinary Cities: Between Modernity and Development*, 168–69. See also Boaventura de Souza Santos, "From the Postmodern to the Postcolonial—and beyond Both," in *Decolonizing European Sociology*, ed. Encarnación Gutiérrez Rodríguez, Manuela Boatca, and Sérgio Costa, 225–42 (London: Ashgate, 2010).

34. Murray, "The Spatial Dynamics of Postmodern Urbanism."

35. Mbembe and Nuttall, "Writing the World from an African Metropolis."

36. Arjun Appadurai and Carol Breckenridge, "Afterword: The Risk of Johannesburg," in *Johannesburg: The Elusive Metropolis*, ed. Sarah Nuttall and Achille Mbembe (Durham: Duke University Press, 2008), 353.

37. Pieterse, "Grasping the Unknowable"; Simone, *City Life from Jakarta to Dakar*; Nuttall, *Entanglement*; Achille Mbembe and Sarah Nuttall, "Introduction: Afropolis," in *Johannesburg: The Elusive Metropolis*, ed. Sarah Nuttall and Achille Mbembe, 1–33 (Durham: Duke University Press, 2008); AbdouMaliq Simone, *For the City Yet to Come: Changing African Life in Four Cities* (Durham: Duke University Press, 2004); Filip de Boeck, "Kinshasa: Tales of the 'Invisible

City' and the Second World," in *Under Siege: Four African Cities. Freetown, Johannesburg, Kinshasa, Lagos. Documenta 11_Platform4*, ed. Okwui Enwezor et al., 243–85 (Ostfildern-Ruit: Hatje Cantz Publishers, 2002); Karen Rodriguez, "Mapping Desire and Transgression through Other Languages: Sex and the (Occasionally Multilingual) Provincial City," *Reconstruction* 11, no. 1 (2011): http://reconstruction.eserver.org/Issues/111/Rodriguez.shtml.

38. Edgar Pieterse, "Exploratory Notes on African Urbanism," paper presented at the European Conference on African Studies, University of Leipzig, June 6, 2009, 5.

39. eThekwini Municipality, Strategic Projects Unit. Durban—Host City: The Warmest Place to Be (Durban, 2009); eThekwini Municipality, Strategic Projects Unit. We Are Durban: Durban Information Guide (Durban, 2009). eThekwini, created in 2000, is the metropolitan municipality that includes the city of Durban and surrounding towns.

40. Elena Bregin, "That's Durban," in *Durban in a Word: Contrasts and Colours in eThekwini*, ed. Dianne Steward (Johannesburg: Penguin Books, 2008), 14.

41. eThekwini Municipality, "EDGE, Economic Development and Growth in eThekwini," issue 4/2012, http://www.durban.gov.za/Resource_Centre/edge/Documents/Edge%20Fast%20Facts%20Issue%204%202012.pdf.

42. Statistics South Africa, "eThekwini," http://beta2.statssa.gov.za/?page_id=1021&id=ethekwini-municipality.

43. See eThekwini Municipality, *eThekwini Quality of Life: Household Survey 2010–2011. A Survey of Municipal Services and Living Conditions* (2011), 38, 39. According to municipal statistics for the entire eThekwini municipality, 2,046 people were murdered between April 2008 and March 2009, a number that has been decreasing since then (1,728 murder victims in 2009/10, and 1,388 for 2010/11). The murder rate per 100,000 persons for eThekwini is 39.6. Durban's inner-city police districts had some of the highest murder ratios within the eThekwini municipality (Durban Central Police: 118 per 100,000 and Point Police 65). See eThekwini Municipality, *Crime Trends in Durban: Mapping Crime Totals as Opposed to Crime Ratios* (2012), 11.

44. Imraan Coovadia, "Midnight," in *Load Shedding: Writing on and over the Edge of South Africa*, ed. Liz McGregor and Sarah Nuttall (Johannesburg: Jonathan Ball Publishers, 2009), 49.

45. Ibid., 46. Durban is the African city with the largest Indian population outside of India.

46. Simone, "The Right to the City," 321.

47. Paul Gilroy, "Cosmopolitanism, Blackness, and Utopia: A Conversation with Paul Gilroy," *Transition* 98 (2008), http://philosophyinatimeoferror.com/2010/10/23/interview-between-tommie-shelby-and-paul-gilroy-class-post/.

48. Comaroff and Comaroff, "Law and Disorder in the Postcolony," 6.

49. Comaroff and Comaroff, *Theory from the South*, 15.

50. Robinson, *Ordinary Cities*.

51. Colin McFarlane, "Urban Shadows: Materiality, the 'Southern City' and Urban Theory," *Geography Compass* 2, no. 2 (2008): 340–58; Roy, "The 21st Century Metropolis," 820; George Marcus, "Ethnography in/of the World System: The Emergence of Multi-sited Ethnography," *Annual Review of Anthropology* 24 (1995): 95–117.

52. Jean Comaroff and John L. Comaroff, "Ethnography on an Awkward Scale: Postcolonial Anthropology and the Violence of Abstraction," *Ethnography* 4, no. 2 (2003): 158.

53. Benoît Dupont, "Mapping Security Networks: From Metaphorical Concept to Empirical Model," in *Fighting Crime Together: The Challenges of Policing and Security Networks*, ed. Jenny Flemming and Jennifer Wood (Sydney: University of New South Wales Press, 2006), 51.

54. Nigel Thrift, "Movement-Space: The Changing Domain of Thinking Resulting from the Development of New Kinds of Spatial Awareness," *Economy and Society* 33, no. 4 (2004): 582–604.

55. Pat O'Malley and Darren Palmer, "Post-Keynesian Policing," *"Economy and Society* 25, no. 2 (1996): 137–55; Nikolas Rose and Peter Miller, "Political Power beyond the State: Problematics of Government," *"British Journal of Sociology* 43, no. 2 (1992): 173–205; Nikolas Rose, *Powers of Freedom: Reframing Political Thought* (Cambridge: Cambridge University Press, 1999); David Garland, "The Limits of the Sovereign State: Strategies of Crime Control in Contemporary Society," *British Journal of Criminology* 36, no. 4 (1996): 445–71; Tania Murray Li, *The Will to Improve: Governmentality, Development, and the Practice of Politics* (Durham: Duke University Press, 2007).

56. Simone, *For the City Yet to Come*; Pieterse, "Grasping the Unknowable"; AbdouMaliq Simone, "Pirate Towns: Reworking Social and Symbolic Infrastructures in Johannesburg and Douala," *Urban Studies* 43, no. 2 (2006): 357–70; Brian Larkin, *Signal and Noise: Media, Infrastructure, and Urban Nigeria* (Durham: Duke University Press, 2008); Filip De Boeck and Marie-Françoise Plissart, *Kinshasa: Tales of the Invisible City* (Gent/Tervuren: Ludion, 2004).

57. James Holston and Teresa Caldeira, "Urban Peripheries and the Invention of Citizenship," *Harvard Design Magazine*, Spring/Summer 2008, 17–23; Marisol García, "Citizenship Practices and Urban Governance in European Cities," *Urban Studies* 43, no. 4 (2006): 745–65; Engin F. Isin and Greg M. Nilesen, *Acts of Citizenship* (London: Zed Books, 2008).

58. Garland, *The Culture of Control*; Feeley and Simon, "The New Penology"; John Adams, *Risk* (London: University College London Press, 1995), 16; Pat O'Malley, "Risk, Power and Crime Prevention," *Economy and Society* 21,

no. 3 (1992): 252- 75; Pat O'Malley, "Risk and Responsibility," in *Foucault and Political Reason: Liberalism, Neo-liberalism, and Rationalities of Government*, ed. Andrew Barry, Thomas Osborne, and Nikolas S. Rose, 189–207 (London: University College London Press, 1996); Shearing and Wood, "Nodal Governance, Denizenship and Communal Space," 201.

59. Daniel M. Goldstein, "Toward a Critical Anthropology of Security," *Current Anthropology* 51, no. 4 (2010): 487. See also Harvey Molotch, *Against Security: How We Go Wrong at Airports, Subways, and Other Sites of Ambiguous Danger* (Princeton: Princeton University Press, 2012).

60. Jonathan Simon, *Governing through Crime: How the War on Crime Transformed American Democracy and Created a Culture of Fear* (Oxford: Oxford University Press, 2007); Mariana Valverde, "Governing Security, Governing through Security," in *The Security of Freedom: Essays on Canada's Anti-Terrorism Bill*, ed. Ronald J. Daniels, Patrick Macklem, and Kent Roach, 83–92 (Toronto: University of Toronto Press, 2001).

61. Austin Zeiderman, "Living Dangerously: Biopolitics and Urban Citizenship in Bogotá, Colombia," *American Ethnologist* 40, no. 1 (2013): 72.

62. Benjamin Goold, Ian Loader, and Angélica Thumala, "The Banality of Security: The Curious Case of Surveillance Cameras," *British Journal of Criminology* 53, no. 6 (2013): 977–96; Ian Loader, "The Anti-Politics of Crime (Review Essay)," *Theoretical Criminology* 12, no. 13 (2008): 399–410.

63. Michel de Certeau, *The Practice of Everyday Life* (Berkeley: University of California Press, 1988), 96ff; Swati Chattopadhyhay, *Unlearning the City: Infrastructure in a New Optical Field* (Minneapolis: University of Minnesota Press, 2012); Henri Lefebvre, *The Production of Space* (Oxford: Blackwell, 1991).

64. Doreen B. Massey, *For Space* (London: Sage, 2005); Martin Coward, "Between Us in the City: Materiality, Subjectivity, and Community in the Era of Global Urbanization," *Environment and Planning D: Society and Space* 30, no. 3 (2012): 468–81; See also Chattopadhyay, *Unlearning the City.*

65. Gillian Rose, "Performing Space," in *Human Geography Today*, ed. Doreen Massey, John Allen, and Phil Sarre (Cambridge: Polity, 1999), 248.

66. Mariana Valverde, "Seeing Like a City: The Dialectic of Modern and Premodern Ways of Seeing in Urban Governance," *Law and Society Review* 45, no. 2 (2011): 277–312; Mariana Valverde, "Seeing Like a City: Legal Tools of Urban Ordering," Genealogies of the Legal symposium, Irvine, Calif., October 28, 2004.

67. Mariana Valverde, *Law's Dream of a Common Knowledge* (Princeton: Princeton University Press, 2003), 20–22; Thrift, "Movement-Space," 585.

68. Ian Loader and Neil Walker, *Civilizing Security* (Cambridge: Cambridge University Press, 2007).

1. The Politics of Crime and Space in South Africa

1. Anthony Altbeker, *A Country at War with Itself: South Africa's Crisis of Crime* (Johannesburg: Jonathan Ball Publishers, 2007), 35; John and Jean L. Comaroff, "Figuring Crime: Quantifacts and the Production of the Un/Real," *Public Culture* 18, no. 1 (2006): 223; Ann Stoler, "Imperial Debris: Reflections on Ruins and Ruination," *Cultural Anthropology* 23, no. 2 (2008): 195.

2. Stoler, "Imperial Debris," 196.

3. Tony Roshan Samara, *Cape Town after Apartheid: Crime and Governance in the Divided City* (Minneapolis: University of Minnesota Press, 2011).

4. Altbeker, *A Country at War with Itself.*

5. Sarah Nuttall, "I Love You, I Hate You," in *Load Shedding: Writing on and over the Edge of South Africa*, ed. Liz McGregor and Sarah Nuttall (Johannesburg: Jonathan Ball Publishers, 2009), 241.

6. Comaroff and Comaroff, "Figuring Crime," 211.

7. Ibid., 209, 211.

8. South African Police Service 2009, "Annual Report: 1 April 2008–31 March 2009," 15; Johan Burger, "A Golden Goal for South Africa: Security Arrangements for the 2010 FIFA Soccer World Cup," *SA Crime Quarterly* 19 (2007): 2.

9. In South Africa, taking the figures from 2006, the murder rate is 41 victims per 100,000 people, which is twenty times higher than that in Western Europe and eight times higher than in the United States. Latin American countries seem to be the only ones to reach or top South African levels of violent crime. Indeed, an international study by Brazilian research group Ritla suggests that El Salvador heads the world's murder statistics with an annual murder rate of 48.8 per 100,000 people, followed by Columbia with 43.8 murder victims per 100,000. See Altbeker, *A Country at War with Itself*, 41f.; Rede de Informacao Tecnológica Latino-Americana, Mapa da Violência: Os Jovens da América Latina—2008, http://www.ritla.org.br/index.php?option=com_content&task=blogcategory&id=0&Itemid=315; Mark Shaw, *Crime and Policing in Post-apartheid South Africa: Transforming under Fire* (Bloomington: Indiana University Press, 2002), 19; John L. and Jean Comaroff, "Law and Disorder in the Postcolony: An Introduction," in *Law and Disorder in the Postcolony*, ed. Jean Comaroff and John L. Comaroff (Chicago: University of Chicago Press, 2006), vii.

10. Altbeker, *A Country at War with Itself*, 33.

11. See Mia Malen, "Creating a New Normal for SA's Men," *Mail and Guardian*, February 22, 2013, 7.

12. Robert Mattes, "Good News and Bad: Public Perceptions of Crime, Corruption and Government," *SA Crime Quarterly* 18 (2006): 11.

13. Comaroff and Comaroff, "Figuring Crime," 211.

14. Interview with prosecutor of the National Prosecution Authority, June 5, 2007, Durban.

15. Ted Legget, "Improved Crime Reporting: Is South Africa's Crime Wave a Statistical Illusion?," *SA Crime Quarterly* 1 (2002): 1–3.

16. Sello S. Alcock, "Crime Stats Scam Exposed," *Mail and Guardian*, July 5, 2009, 14.

17. Comaroff and Comaroff, "Figuring Crime," 210.

18. Ibid., 211.

19. Tshwete justified the moratorium by the inaccuracy and unreliability of the numbers released by the South African Police Service (SAPS) and presented a plan to revise the procedures of data collection, but the moratorium was lifted a year later. See also: Tony Roshan Samara, "State Security in Transition: The War on Crime in Post Apartheid South Africa," *Social Identities* 9, no. 2 (2003): 285; Comaroff and Comaroff, "Figuring Crime," 221; Legget, "Improved Crime Reporting."

20. "DA slams Cele over Crime Statistics," *Mail and Guardian*, August 4, 2009, http://www.mg.co.za/article/2009-08-04-da-slams-cele-over-crime -statistics.

21. "Editorial Comment: This Is a Crisis, Not Just a Problem," *Sunday Times*, October 1, 2006, 1.

22. Ibid.

23. Deborah Posel, Julia Hornberger, and Achille Mbembe, "Crime and Politics in Our Time," *Wiser Review* no. 3 (2008): 8.

24. Ibid.

25. Ibid. On successful crime fighting as crucial to the legitimacy of the South African democracy, see also Bruce Baker, *Taking the Law into Their Own Hands: Lawless Law Enforcers in Africa* (Aldershot: Ashgate, 2002); Samara, "State Security in Transition"; Shaw, *Crime and Policing in Post-apartheid South Africa*.

26. Posel, Hornberger and Mbembe, "Crime and Politics in Our Time," 8.

27. Ibid., 9.

28. Gary Kynoch, "Apartheid Nostalgia: Personal Security Concerns in South African Townships, South Africa," *SA Crime Quarterly* 5 (2003): 7–10.

29. Ibid., 8.

30. According to the Pass Law Act from 1952, all South Africans categorized as African, Coloured, or Indian over the age of sixteen had to carry pass books, which regulated, amongst many things, their movements from a nonwhite to a white area and their permission to take and change jobs. Not carrying one's pass book or not possessing the valid entry in it was cause for arrest and led to the imprisonment of millions of black South Africans. See Deborah Posel, *The Making of Apartheid, 1948–1961: Conflict and Compromise* (Oxford: Clarendon Press, 1991), 5.

31. Kynoch, "Apartheid Nostalgia," 10.

32. See, e.g., Shaw, *Crime and Policing in Post-Apartheid South Africa*; Gary Kynoch, *We Are Fighting the World: A History of the Marashea Gangs in South Africa, 1947–1999* (Athens: Ohio University Press; Pietermaritzburg: University of KwaZulu-Natal Press, 2005); Shula Marks and Neil Andersson, "The Epidemiology and Culture of Violence," in *Political Violence and the Struggle in South Africa*, ed. N. Chabani Manganyi and André du Toit, 29–69 (Halfway House, S.A.: Southern Book Publishers, 1990); Clive Glaser, "Whistles and Sjamboks: Crime and Policing in Soweto, 1960–1976," *South African Historical Journal* 52 (2005): 119–39.

33. Kynoch, "Apartheid Nostalgia," 10.

34. Interview with beach security manager, June 2, 2007, Durban.

35. Ian Hacking, "How Should We Do the History of Statistics?" in *The Foucault Effect: Studies in Governmentality: With Two Lectures by and an Interview with Michel Foucault*, ed. Graham Burchell, Colin Gordon, and Peter Miller, 15–26 (Chicago: University of Chicago Press, 1991); Michel Foucault, *Il Faut Défendre la Société: Cours au Collège de France (1975–1976)* (Paris: Gallimard Seuil, 1997), 216 ff; Michel Foucault, "Polémique, Politique et Problematisations (entretien avec P. Rabinow)," in *Dits et Ecrits 1954–1988*, vol. 4, ed. Daniel Defert and Francois Ewald, 591–608 (Paris: Gallimard, 1994); Michel Foucault, "Questions of Method," in *The Foucault Effect: Studies in Governmentality: With Two Lectures by and an Interview with Michel Foucault*, ed. Graham Burchell, Colin Gordon, and Peter Miller, 73–86 (Chicago: University of Chicago Press, 1991); Kevin D. Haggerty, *Making Crime Count* (Toronto: University of Toronto Press, 2001).

36. Slabbert, cited in Marks and Andersson, "The Epidemiology and Culture of Violence," 55.

37. Lucia Zedner, *Criminal Justice* (Oxford: Oxford University Press, 2004), 39f; Mariana Valverde, *Law and Order: Images, Meanings, Myths* (New Brunswick: Rutgers University Press, 2006).

38. Shaw, *Crime and Policing in Post-Apartheid South Africa*, 1. I use the term "black" for all those people categorized and discriminated against as "African," "Coloured," or "Indian" under the apartheid regime, as defined by the Population Registration Act of 1950. The apartheid state enfranchised whites as citizens and disenfranchised blacks as noncitizens. Often, the apartheid government used the word "black" for Africans only. In contrast, the antiapartheid movement led by Steve Biko in the 1970s and 1980s used the term "black" as an overarching term that incorporated Coloureds, Indians, and Africans, highlighting the political determinates of race and the need to fight racial discrimination together. Being black, in Steve Biko's terms, referred both to suffering from racial oppression and to fighting against it. Blackness, in this sense, was a

positive racial consciousness. Those who were discriminated against but did not challenge it were defined negatively as "nonwhites." The new democratic South African constitution from 1996 declares all discrimination on the basis of race illegal. However, in postapartheid South Africa, the use of categories created during apartheid remains widespread, both in popular and official language. These classifications are the basis for administrative regulations aimed at redressing former injustice by bringing those who had previously been classified and discriminated against as African, Indian, or Coloured into better professional positions. See Michael MacDonald, *Why Race Matters in South Africa* (Cambridge, Mass.: Harvard University Press, 2006), 2, 118.

39. Rosalind C. Morris, "The Spectral Police: A South African Story," paper presented at the annual meeting of the American Anthropological Association, Washington, D.C., December 2, 2005; Jean and John Comaroff, "Detective Fictions and Sovereign Pursuits: Further Adventures in Policing the Postcolony," paper presented at the Bayreuth International School of African Studies, University of Bayreuth; Bayreuth, Germany, November 18, 2009. Shaw, *Crime and Policing in Post-Apartheid South Africa*, 1, 15; William Beinart, "Political and Collective Violence in Southern African Historiography," *Journal of Southern African Studies* 18, no. 3 (1991): 455–86.

40. Comaroff and Comaroff, "Figuring Crime," 220; MacDonald, *Why Race Matters in South Africa*, 13.

41. Clifford Shearing and Julie Berg, "South Africa," in *Plural Policing: A Comparative Perspective*, ed. Trevor Jones and Tim Newburn (London: Routledge, 2006), 197; Shaw, *Crime and Policing in Post-apartheid South Africa*, 15.

42. See Shaw, *Crime and Policing in Post-apartheid South Africa*, 3; Kynoch, *We Are Fighting the World*; Gary Kynoch, "From the Ninevites to the Hard Livings Gang: Township Gangsters and Urban Violence in Twentieth-Century South Africa," *African Studies* 58, no. 1 (1999): 55–85; Marks and Andersson, "The Epidemiology and Culture of Violence."

43. Kynoch, "From the Ninevites to the Hard Livings Gang," 58–59.

44. Altbeker, *A Country at War with Itself*; Legget, "Improved Crime Reporting"; Samara, "State Security in Transition."

45. Shaw, *Crime and Policing in Post-Apartheid South Africa*, 3; SAIRR (South African Institute of Race Relations). "A Survey of Race Relations, 1977," 1978, Johannesburg.

46. Interview with manager of the Department of Community Safety and Liaison, Province of KwaZulu-Natal, June 4, 2007, Pietermaritzburg.

47. Comaroff and Comaroff, "Figuring Crime," 220–21.

48. Until 2001 the Medical Research Council published the racial profile of murder victims. The 2001 report states that less than 5 percent of murder victims are white (against their 10 percent share of the population). "Indians" and

women were also relationally underrepresented. See Altbeker, *A Country at War with Itself*, 62.

49. Ibid., 63.

50. Jean and John Comaroff, "Criminal Obsessions, after Foucault: Post-coloniality, Policing, and the Metaphysics of Disorder," *Critical Inquiry* 30 (2004): 804.

51. Interview with Point police officer, March 20, 2006, Durban. See also Frederick Schauer, *Profiles, Probabilities, and Stereotypes* (Cambridge, Mass.: Harvard University Press, 2003), 196; see also Oscar H. Gandy Jr., "Quixotics Unite! Engaging the Pragmatics on Rational Discrimination," in *Theorizing Surveillance: The Panopticon and Beyond*, ed. David Lyon (Cullompton, U.K.: Willan Publishing, 2006), 330; David Lyon, "Surveillance as Social Sorting: Computer Codes and Mobile Bodies," in *Surveillance as Social Sorting: Privacy, Risk, and Digital Discrimination*, ed. David Lyon, 1–9 (London: Routledge, 2003).

52. Posel, Hornberger, and Mbembe, "Crime and Politics in Our Time," 8.

53. Cf. Altbeker, *A Country at War with Itself*, 101.

54. Marks and Andersson, "The Epidemiology and Culture of Violence," 32; Shaw, *Crime and Policing in Post-apartheid South Africa*, 3. See also Stephen Ellis, "The New Frontiers of Crime in South Africa," in *The Criminalization of the State in Africa*, ed. Jean-François Bayart, Stephen Ellis, and Béatrice Hibou (Oxford: James Currey, 1999), 61.

55. Marks and Andersson, "The Epidemiology and Culture of Violence."

56. Kynoch, "From the Ninevites to the Hard Livings Gang"; Kynoch, *We Are Fighting the World*; Mac Fenwick, "'Tough Guy, eh?': The Gangster-Figure in Drum," *Journal of Southern African Studies* 22, no. 4 (1996): 617–32.

57. Henry Nxumalo, "The Birth of a Tsotsi," in *The Drum Decade: Stories from the 1950s*, ed. Michael Chapman (Pietermaritzburg: University of KwaZulu-Natal Press, 2001), 21.

58. Fenwick, "'Tough Guy, eh?,'" 620.

59. Ibid., 626.

60. Posel, Hornberger and Mbembe, "Crime and Politics in Our Time"; see also Kynoch, *We Are Fighting the World*.

61. This, as Posel underlines, includes people being convicted several times. Posel, *The Making of Apartheid, 1948–1961*, 120.

62. Kynoch, "From the Ninevites to the Hard Livings Gang"; Jonny Steinberg, *The Number: One Man's Search for Identity in the Cape Underworld and Prison Gangs* (Johannesburg: Jonathan Ball Publishers, 2004).

63. Karima Brown, "South Africa: Death Penalty—Let Country Vote," *Business Day* (2008), http://allafrica.com/stories/200803070487.html. For a general "'get tough' rhetoric of the political elite" from the mid-1990s, see, for example, Samara ("State Security in Transition," 285ff); "Kill the Criminals, Minister Tells Cops," *Mail and Guardian*, April 10, 2008, http://www.mg.co

.za/article/2008-04-10-kill-the-criminals-minister-tells-cops; Mail and Guardian Online, "Zuma Urges Tougher Laws on Crime," *Mail and Guardian*, December 29, 2008, http://www.mg.co.za/article/2008-12-29-zuma-urges-tougher-laws -on-crime.

64. Ian Loader, "Plural Policing and Democratic Governance," *Social and Legal Studies* 9, no. 3 (2000): 323–45; Shearing and Berg, "South Africa"; David Garland, "'Governmentality' and the Problem of Crime: Foucault, Criminology, Sociology," *Theoretical Criminology* 1, no. 2 (1997): 173–214; Pat O'Malley and Darren Palmer, "Post-Keynesian Policing," *Economy and Society* 25, no. 2 (1996): 137–55; Adam Crawford, "Policing and Security as 'Club Goods': The New Enclosures?," in *Democracy, Society and the Governance of Security*, ed. Jennifer Wood and Benoit Dupont (Cambridge: Cambridge University Press, 2006), 123.

65. Shaw, *Crime and Policing in Post-Apartheid South Africa*, 13.

66. Glaser, "Whistles and Sjamboks," 124; Gavin Cawthra, *Policing South Africa: The South African Police and the Transition from Apartheid* (London: Zed Books, 1993), 9.

67. In the early 1970s South Africa's police killed an average of 84 people a year, which was double the rate of police killings in the United States. After the Soweto uprisings in 1976, the annual rate increased dramatically, ranging from a low of 163 in 1979 to 763 in 1985 (deaths in police custody not included). See Cawthra, *Policing South Africa*, 2; Monique Marks, *Transforming the Robocops: Changing Police in South Africa* (Pietermaritzburg: University of KwaZulu-Natal Press, 2005); Monique Marks, "Changing Dilemmas and the Dilemmas of Change: Transforming the Public Order Police Unit in Durban," *Policing and Society* 9, no. 2 (1999): 157–79; Monique Marks, "Changing Police, Policing Change: The Case of Kwazulu Natal," *Society in Transition* no. 1 (1997): 54–69; Shearing and Berg, "South Africa," 197.

68. Marks, "Changing Police, Policing Change"; Elrena van der Spuy, "South African Policing Studies in the Making," in *Justice Gained? Crime and Crime Control in South Africa's Transition*, ed. Bill Dixon and Elrena van der Spuy (Cape Town: UCT Press; Willan Publishing, 2004), 210 ff.; Bill Dixon, "Cosmetic Crime Prevention," in *Justice Gained? Crime and Crime Control in South Africa's Transition*, ed. Bill Dixon and Elrena van der Spuy (Cape Town: UCT Press; Willan Publishing, 2004), 164ff.

69. Marks, "Changing Police, Policing Change"; Steffen Jensen and Lars Buur, "Everyday Policing and the Occult: Notions of Witchcraft, Crime and 'the People,'"*African Studies* 63, no. 2 (2004): 209; Steffen Jensen, "Claiming Community: Government, Township Politics, and the Specter of Crime," IIS/GI, Kongevej Working Paper, Institute for International Studies, Copenhagen 03, no. 4 (2003): 2.

70. Shearing and Berg, "South Africa," 198.

71. See the SAPS website at http://www.saps.gov.za.

72. Mari Harris and Stephano Radaelli, "Paralysed by Fear: Perceptions of Crime and Violence in South Africa," *SA Crime Quarterly* 20 (2007): 4.

73. Bruce Baker, "Living with Non-State Policing in South Africa: The Issues and Dilemmas," *Journal of Modern African Studies* 40, no. 1 (2002): 32, 33.

74. In KwaZulu, the "Zulu Homeland," "conservative vigilante 'warriors' mobs" formed in the context of the Inkatha Freedom Party (IFP) and attacked students involved in school boycotts and other antiapartheid protests during the 1980s. The Inkatha Freedom Party was founded in 1975 by chief Mangosuthu Buthelezi, who was also the head of KwaZulu and who leads the party up until today. The IFP grounds itself in values of conservative "Zuluness" and partly cooperated with the apartheid regime. The South African state at the time provided these anti-UDF militias with arms and support. During South Africa's period of transition to democracy in the 1990s, Buthelezi called for a fight against the ANC, and a wave of violence broke out, in which seven thousand people lost their lives, mostly in KwaZulu-Natal. See Nicholas Haysom, "Mabangalala: The Rise of Right-Wing Vigilantes in South Africa," *Occasional Paper No. 10* (Centre for Applied Legal Studies, University of the Witwatersrand, 1986), 84ff, 113ff; Ellis, "The New Frontiers of Crime in South Africa," 61; Baker, *Taking the Law into Their Own Hands*, 56.

75. Glaser, "Whistles and Sjamboks," 128f.

76. Michael Kempa and Clifford Shearing, "Microscopic and Macroscopic Responses to Inequalities in the Governance of Security: Respective Experiments in South Africa and Northern Ireland," *Transformation* 49 (2002): 31; David H. Bayley and Clifford D. Shearing, "The Future of Policing," *Law and Society Review* 30, no. 3 (1996): 585–606.

77. Shearing and Berg, "South Africa," 202.

78. Kempa and Shearing, "Microscopic and Macroscopic Responses to Inequalities," 32, 46; see also Clifford Shearing and Jennifer Wood, "Nodal Governance, Denizenship and Communal Space: Challenges to the Westphalian Ideal," in *Limits to Liberation after Apartheid: Citizenship, Governance and Culture*, ed. Steven Robins, 97–112 (Oxford: James Currey, 2005); Martin Murray, "The Spatial Dynamics of Postmodern Urbanism: Social Polarisation and Fragmentation in Sao Paulo and Johannesburg," *Journal of Contemporary African Studies* 22, no. 2 (2004): 139–64; Steven Robins, "At the Limits of Spatial Governmentality: A Message from the Tip of Africa," *Third World Quarterly* 23, no. 4 (2002): 665–89; Samara, *Cape Town after Apartheid*.

79. PSIRA 2009: Annual Report 2008/2009, 29.

80. Michael Kempa and Anne-Marie Singh, "Private Security, Political Economy and the Policing of Race: Probing Global Hypotheses through the Case of South Africa," *Theoretical Criminology* 12, no. 3 (2008): 343.

81. Adam Crawford, "Policing and Security as 'Club Goods': The New Enclosures?," in *Democracy, Society and the Governance of Security*, ed. Jennifer Wood and Benoit Dupont (Cambridge: Cambridge University Press, 2006), 123; Faranak Miraftab, "Governing Post Apartheid Spatiality: Implementing City Improvement Districts in Cape Town," *Antipode* 39, no. 4 (2007): 602–26; Martin Murray, *Taming the Disorderly City: The Spatial Landscape of Johannesburg after Apartheid* (Ithaca: Cornell University Press, 2008).

82. Shearing and Berg, "South Africa," 205.

83. Lars Buur and Steffen Jensen, "Introduction: Vigilantism and the Policing of Everyday Life in South Africa," *African Studies* 63, no. 2 (2004): 139–52; Ashwin Desai, "The Cape of Good Dope? A Post-Apartheid Story of Gangs and Vigilantes," research report for the Centre for Civil Society and the School of Development Studies University of KwaZulu-Natal (2004); Baker, *Taking the Law into Their Own Hands*, 155; Shearing and Berg, "South Africa"; Sindre Bangstad, "Hydra's Heads: PAGAD and Responses to the PAGAD Phenomenon in a Cape Muslim Community," *Journal of Southern African Studies* 31, no. 1 (2005): 178–208; Daniel Nina, "Popular Justice in the 'New South Africa': From People's Courts to Community Courts in Alexandra," Occasional Paper 15 CALS, Wits University, Johannesburg, March 1992.

84. Buur and Jensen, "Introduction," 148.

85. Jonny Steinberg, *Thin Blue: The Unwritten Rules of Policing South Africa* (Johannesburg: Jonathan Ball; Open Society Foundation for South Africa, 2008), 176; see also Shearing and Berg, "South Africa," 208.

86. Patrick Bond, *Elite Transition: From Apartheid to Neoliberalism in South Africa* (Pietermaritzburg: University of KwaZulu-Natal Press, 2005); Patrick Bond, "South Africa's Frustrating Decade of Freedom: From Racial to Class Apartheid," *Monthly Review* 55, no. 10 (2004): 45–59; Ashwin Desai, *We Are the Poors: Community Struggles in Post-Apartheid South Africa* (New York: Monthly Review Press, 2002); Michael Hardt, "Foreword: What Affects Are Good For," in *The Affective Turn: Theorizing the Social*, ed. Patricia Ticineto Clough and Jean Halley, ix–xiii (Durham: Duke University Press, 2007); Miraftab, "Governing Post Apartheid Spatiality."

87. Edgar Pieterse, "Post-Apartheid Geographies in South Africa: Why Are Urban Divides So Persistent?," paper presented at the workshop Interdisciplinary Debates on Development and Cultures: Cities in Development—Spaces, Conflicts and Agency, Leuven University, December 13, 2009, 1.

88. Achille Mbembe, "Aesthetics of Superfluity," *Public Culture* 16, no. 3 (2004): 386.

89. The 1913 Land Act prohibited Africans from buying land in white rural areas. The 1923 Urban Areas Act denied Africans the right to hold title in municipal townships. And the 1937 Native Laws Amendment Act prohibited Africans

from the purchase of landed property in urban areas outside the reserves. See Paul Maylam, "Introduction: The Struggle for Space in Twentieth-Century Durban," in *The People's City: African Life in Twentieth-Century Durban*, ed. Paul Maylam and Iain Edwards (Pietermaritzburg: University of Natal Press, 1996), 9.

90. When the Group Areas Act in 1950 was introduced at a national level, the Durban Corporation was enthusiastic, since local plans for racial segregation were already in the making. In fact, as Brij Maharaj has pointed out, the Durban Corporation was a prime motivator for the Group Areas Act. The Durban riots in 1949, where groups of Africans attacked Indian people and property throughout the city, especially in Cato Manor, and during which 142 people were killed, were in some regard seen as the proof for the wisdom underlying the Group Areas Act. See Brij Maharaj, "The Historical Development of the Apartheid Local State in South Africa: The Case of Durban," *International Journal of Urban and Regional Research* 20, no. 4 (1996): 587–600; E. Jeffrey Popke, "Violence and Memory in the Reconstruction of South Africa's Cato Manor," *Growth and Change* 31, no. 2 (2000): 242.

91. The criteria for classification were based on physical appearance and social acceptability. The rationale was to prevent people who were neither recognizable nor socially acceptable as white persons from gaining the status of "white." However, during apartheid, several thousand people changed classifications. As Christopher calculates, between 1983 and 1990 alone, seven thousand people had their racial description changed. See Anthony J. Christopher, *The Atlas of Changing South Africa* (New York: Routledge, 2001), 101, 102.

92. Under the prohibitions of the Mixed Marriage Act (1949) and the Immorality Amendment Act (1950). See also ibid., 102.

93. Ibid., 103.

94. Popke, "Violence and Memory," 242ff; Bill Freund, "Contrasts in Urban Segregation: A Tale of Two African Cities, Durban (South Africa) and Abidjan (Côte d'Ivoire)," *Journal of Southern African Studies* 27, no. 3 (2001): 531.

95. Christopher, *The Atlas of Changing South Africa*, 130; Maynard Swanson, "'The Asiatic Menace': Creating Segregation in Durban, 1870–1900," *International Journal of African Historical Studies* 16, no. 3 (1983): 404.

96. This was codified in the Separate Amenities Act (1953).

97. Frantz Fanon, *Les damnés de la Terre* (Paris: Gallimard, 1991), 82; Achille Mbembe, "Necropolitics," *Public Culture* 15, no. 1 (2003): 26, 27.

98. Mbembe, "Aesthetics of Superfluity," 389. In Durban the KwaZulu Homeland was given nominal independence and control over the vast townships KwaMashu and Umlazi in 1974. Borders were gerrymandered in order to make African townships fall under the control of the KwaZulu Bantustan. By the early '70s, no African township formally belonged to the city of Durban

anymore. Most of Durban's African residents consequently became cross-border commuters. See Michael Sutcliffe, "The Fragmented City: Durban, South Africa," *International Social Science Journal, UNESCO* 48, no. 1 (1996): 68; Popke, "Violence and Memory," 243.

99. Achille Mbembe, "Aesthetics of Superfluity," 389.

100. See Posel, *The Making of Apartheid, 1948–1961*, 66–67.

101. Ibid., 75–76.

102. Ibid., 76.

103. The control of influx also implied a sharp increase in policing. The SAP grew from 14,743 members in 1946 to 23,016 in 1955, most of whom were placed in white areas. Additional black police were employed to police influx offenses. Within township boundaries, African constables were given the power to arrest without a warrant (ibid., 119).

104. Fanon, *Les Damnés de la Terre*, 82.

105. Posel, *The Making of Apartheid, 1948–1961*, 5. Apartheid influx control was regulated by the 1952 Native Laws Amendment Act together with the Abolition of Passes and Documents Act (ibid., 111).

106. G. H. Pirie, "Travelling under Apartheid," in *The Apartheid City and Beyond: Urbanization and Social Change in South Africa*, ed. David, M. Smith (London: Routledge 1992), 173.

107. Mbembe, "Aesthetics of Superfluity," 387.

108. Ibid., 387.

109. Mbembe, "Necropolitics," 27; Foucault, *Il Faut Défendre la Société*, 228.

110. Foucault, *Il Faut Défendre la Société*, 228, 229.

111. Mbembe, "Necropolitics," 39.

112. Mbembe, "Aesthetics of Superfluity," 384.

113. Ibid., 384.

114. Judith Butler, *Frames of War: When Is Life Grievable?* (London: Verso, 2009), 4.

115. Ibid., 31.

116. Zygmunt Bauman, *Liquid Modernity* (Cambridge: Polity, 2000), 95.

117. Mbembe, "Aesthetics of Superfluity," 391.

118. David Lyon, *Surveillance Studies: An Overview* (Cambridge: Polity, 2007), 98.

119. Sarah Nuttall, *Entanglement: Literary and Cultural Reflections on Post-Apartheid* (Johannesburg: Wits University Press, 2009), 114.

120. Edgar Pieterse, "Building with Ruins and Dreams: Some Thoughts on Realising Integrated Urban Development in South Africa through Crisis," *Urban Studies* 43, no. 2 (2006): 286.

121. Interview with traffic planner, eThekwini Transport Authority, September 29, 2007, Durban.

122. Interview with municipal architect, June 5, 2007, Durban.

123. Ibid.

124. Interview with beach security manager, April 23, 2008, Durban. The Wheel is a downtown shopping center built in 1989 as a beacon of white consumerist modernity close to the beachfront and in the middle of the now notorious Point Road area. During the decade of the South African transition, it suffered from "urban degeneration," with many shops staying vacant. The Wheel has recently become China Mall.

125. Interview with municipal architect.

126. Interview with city manager, June 8, 2007, Durban.

127. Maylam, "Introduction," 26.

128. AbdouMaliq Simone, "The Right to the City," *Interventions* 7, no. 3 (2005): 321, 322.

129. Sarah Nuttall, "Literary City," in *Johannesburg: The Elusive Metropolis*, ed. Sarah Nuttall and Achille Mbembe (Durham: Duke University Press, 2008), 198; Jo Beall, Owen Crankshaw and Sue Parnell, *Uniting a Divided City: Governance and Social Exclusion in Johannesburg* (London: Earthscan Publications, 2002); Steven Robins, "At the Limits of Spatial Governmentality: A Message from the Tip of Africa," *Third World Quarterly* 23, no. 4 (2002): 656–89; Lindsay Bremner, "Closure, Simulation and Making-Do in the Contemporary Johannesburg Landscape," in *Under Siege: Four African Cities. Freetown, Johannesburg, Kinshasa, Lagos. Documenta 11_Platform4*, ed. Okwui Enwezor, Carlos Basualdo, Uta Meta Bauer, Susanne Ghez, Sarat Maharaj, Mark Nash, and Octavio Zaya (Ostfildern-Ruit: Hatje Cantz, 2002): 153–72.

130. Imraan Coovadia, *High Low In-Between* (Roggebaai: Umuzi, 2009), 135f.

131. Ibid., 135.

132. Nuttall, "Literary City"; Robins, "At the Limits of Spatial Governmentality."

133. Ivan Vladislavic, *Portrait with Keys: Joburg and What-What* (Roggebaai, South Africa: Umuzi, 2006), 11.

134. Miraftab, "Governing Post Apartheid Spatiality"; Murray, *Taming the Disorderly City*; Gillian Hart, "The Provocations of Neoliberalism: Contesting the Nation and Liberation after Apartheid," *Antipode* 40, no. 4 (2008), 678–705; Bond, "South Africa's Frustrating Decade of Freedom," 45-59; Samara, *Cape Town after Apartheid*; Pieterse, "Building with Ruins and Dreams."

135. Bond, "South Africa's Frustrating Decade of Freedom."

136. Murray, *Taming the Disorderly City*, 26; Miraftab, "Governing Post Apartheid Spatiality"; Faranak Miraftab, "Making Neo-liberal Governance: The Disempowering Work of Empowerment," *International Planning Studies* 9, no. 4 (2007): 239–60.

2. Seeing Like a City

1. Mariana Valverde, "Governing Security, Governing through Security," in *The Security of Freedom: Essays on Canada's Anti-Terrorism Bill*, ed. Ronald J. Daniels, Patrick Macklem, and Kent Roach (Toronto: University of Toronto Press, 2001), 85.

2. Mariana Valverde, "Seeing Like a City: The Dialectic of Modern and Premodern Ways of Seeing in Urban Governance," *Law and Society Review* 45, no. 2 (2011): 277–31; Mariana Valverde, *Law's Dream of a Common Knowledge* (Princeton: Princeton University Press, 2003), 2–4, 20–22; Nigel Thrift, "Movement-Space: The Changing Domain of Thinking Resulting from the Development of New Kinds of Spatial Awareness," *Economy and Society* 33, no. 4 (2004): 585.

3. Lucia Zedner demarcates a distinction between security as a "state of being" versus a "means to that end." As a means, security is understood as a process in which a goal with the same name, security, is pursued. "The pursuit of security," Zedner argues, "may be something like an end in itself." Its importance arises out of the fact that security as a goal is almost never achieved absolutely and is continuously challenged by new threats. See Lucia Zedner, "The Concept of Security: An Agenda for Comparative Analysis," *Legal Studies* 23, no. 1 (2003): 155–56; Lucia Zedner, "Policing before and after the Police: The Historical Antecedents of Contemporary Crime Control," *British Journal of Criminology* 46, no. 1 (2006): 82; Lucia Zedner, *Security* (New York: Routledge, 2009).

4. Nikolas Rose and Mariana Valverde, "Governed by Law?," *Social and Legal Studies* 7, no. 4 (1998): 545. See also Tania Murray Li, "Practices of Assemblage and Community Forest Management," *Economy and Society* 36, no. 2 (2007): 264; Michel Foucault, "Polémique, Politique et Problematisations (entretien avec P. Rabinow)," and "Usage des Plaisirs et Techniques de Soi," both in *Dits et Ecrits 1954–1988*, vol. 4, ed. Daniel Defert and Francois Ewald, 591–608, 539–65 (Paris: Gallimard, 1994); Michel Foucault, in *Dits et Ecrits 1954–1988, vol. IV*, ed. Daniel Defert and Francois Ewald (Paris: Gallimard, 1994).

5. Michel Foucault, "The Subject and Power," in *Michel Foucault: Beyond Structuralism and Hermeneutics*, ed. Hubert L. Dreyfus and Paul Rabinow (Chicago: University of Chicago Press, 1982), 221.

6. See also Collin Gordon, "Governmental Rationality: An Introduction," in *The Foucault Effect: Studies in Governmentality; With Two Lectures by and an Interview with Michel Foucault*, ed. Graham Burchell, Colin Gordon, and Peter Miller (Chicago: University of Chicago Press, 1991): 2; Alan Hunt and Gary Wickham, *Foucault and Law: Towards a Sociology of Law as Governance* (London: Pluto Press, 1994), 23–24.

7. Sally Engle Merry, "Spatial Governmentality and the New Urban Social Order: Controlling Gender Violence through Law," *American Anthropologist* 103, no. 1 (2001): 18; Valverde, *Law's Dream of a Common Knowledge*, 12.

8. Valverde, "Governing Security, Governing through Security," 89, 91; Jonathan Simon, *Governing through Crime: How the War on Crime Transformed American Democracy and Created a Culture of Fear* (Oxford: Oxford University Press, 2007). The idea of governing through crime or governing through security is in fact already inherent in Foucault's work. Foucault lays out in *Discipline and Punish* how the prison fails to reduce illegalities. Yet, this failure is also its success, insofar as it yields dividing practices, including the dangerous from the respectable, the mad from the sane, and so forth. See Michel Foucault, *Discipline and Punish: The Birth of the Prison* (New York: Pantheon Books, 1977); see also Hunt and Wickham, *Foucault and Law*.

9. Clifford Shearing, "Governing Security and Making Space," lecture presented at the workshop Governing Security and Making Space, Freie Universität Berlin, September 5, 2008.

10. See also Rose and Valverde, "Governed by Law?"

11. See Mitchell Dean, *Governmentality: Power and Rule in Modern Society* (London: New Delhi: Sage, 2010); Oscar H. Gandy Jr., *The Panoptic Sort: A Political Economy of Personal Information* (Boulder, Colo.: Westview Press, 1993); Susanne Krasmann, *Die Kriminalität der Gesellschaft: Zur Gouvernementalität der Gegenwart* (Konstanz: UVK, 2003); Simon, *Governing through Crime*; Rose and Valverde, "Governed by Law?"; Valverde, *Law's Dream of a Common Knowledge*.

12. David Lyon, *Surveillance Studies: An Overview* (Cambridge: Polity, 2007), 98.

13. Katherine Beckett and Steve Herbert, "Dealing with Disorder: Social Control in the Post-Industrial City," *Theoretical Criminology* 12, no. 1 (2008): 5–30.

14. Mariana Valverde, "Analyzing the Governance of Security: Jurisdiction and Scale," *Behemoth: A Journal on Civilisation* 1, no. 1 (2008): 7.

15. David H. Bayley and Clifford D. Shearing, "The Future of Policing," *Law and Society Review* 30, no. 3 (1996): 585–606; Scott Burris, Michael Kempa, and Clifford Shearing, "Changes in Governance: A Cross-Disciplinary Review of Current Scholarship," *Akron Law Review* 41, no. 1 (2008): 1–66; Adam Crawford, "Networked Governance and the Post-Regulatory State? Steering, Rowing and Anchoring the Provision of Policing and Security," *Theoretical Criminology* 10, no. 4 (2006): 449–79; Hunt and Wickham, *Foucault and Law*, 25; Pat O'Malley, Lorna Weir, and Clifford Shearing, "Governmentalty, Criticism, Politics," *Economy and Society* 26, no. 4 (1997): 501–17; Ulf Engel and Andreas Mehler, "'Under Construction': Governance in Africa's New Violent

Social Spaces," in *The African Exception*, ed. Ulf Engel and Gorm Rye Olsen, 1–13 (Aldershot: Ashgate, 2005); Jennifer Wood and Clifford Shearing, *Imagining Security* (Cullompton, U.K.: Willan Publishing, 2007).

16. Trevor Jones and Tim Newburn, *Private Security and Public Policing* (Oxford: Clarendon Press, 1998), 18.

17. Ian Loader, "Plural Policing and Democratic Governance," *Social and Legal Studies* 9, no. 3 (2000): 323–45; Clifford Shearing and Julie Berg, "South Africa," in *Plural Policing: A Comparative Perspective*, ed. Trevor Jones and Tim Newburn, 190–221 (London: Routledge, 2006).

18. Bruce Baker, *Multi-Choice Policing in Africa* (Uppsala: Nordiska Afrikainstitutet, 2008).

19. Michael D. McGinnis, introduction to *Polycentric Governance and Development: Readings from the Workshop in Political Theory and Policy Analysis*, ed. Michael D. McGinnis, 1–28 (Ann Arbor: University of Michigan Press, 1999); Wood and Shearing, *Imagining Security*.

20. Andreas Mehler, *Legitime Gewaltoligopole—eine Antwort auf strukturelle Instabilität in Westafrika?* (Hamburg: Institut für Afrika-Kunde, 2003). Oligopolies, which can be both functional and territorial, allow one to systematically analyze and map security practices of different agents, such as private security firms, warlords, religious leaders, state actors, or vigilante groups. Borrowing from macro-economic theory, the notion of oligopolies of violence then pays particular attention to the various ways by which these actors share "security markets" between themselves.

21. The concept of nodal governance aims "to denote a multiplicity of governance authorities and providers that co-exist in multiple ways to produce diverse security outcomes." Nodes are "sites of knowledge, capacity and resources that function as governance auspices and providers." Nodes may be linked to one another, or not, they may form part of a hierarchical relationship, or not, and they can be involved in divisions of labor between "rowing and steering." See Wood and Shearing, *Imagining Security*, 13, 27; Les Johnston and Clifford Shearing, *Governing Security: Explorations in Policing and Justice* (London: Routledge, 2003).

22. Colin McFarlane, *Learning the City: Knowledge and Translocal Assemblage,* (Malden, Mass.: Wiley-Blackwell, 2011); Jane Bennett, *Vibrant Matter: A Political Ecology of Things* (Durham: Duke University Press, 2010); Kevin D. Haggerty and Richard V. Ericson, "The Surveillant Assemblage," *British Journal of Sociology* 51, no. 4 (2000): 605–22; Bruno Latour, *Science in Action: How to Follow Scientists and Engineers through Society* (Cambridge, Mass.: Harvard University Press, 1987); Murray Li, "Practices of Assemblage and Community Forest Management."

23. Valverde, "Analyzing the Governance of Security," 8.

24. Valverde, "Seeing Like a City," 309.

25. Ibid., 280–81.

26. Patrick Joyce, *The Rule of Freedom: Liberalism and the Modern City* (London: Verso, 2003); Paul La Hausse, "The Struggle for the City: Alcohol, the Ematsheni and Popular Culture in Durban 1902–1936," in *The People's City: African Life in Twentieth-Century Durban*, ed. Paul Maylam and Iain Edwards, 33–66 (Pietermaritzburg: University of Natal Press, 1996); Alan Hunt, *Governing Morals: A Social History of Moral Regulation* (Cambridge: Cambridge University Press, 1999); Steve Macek, *Urban Nightmares: The Media, the Right, and the Moral Panic over the City* (Minneapolis: University of Minnesota Press, 2006); Martin Murray, *Taming the Disorderly City: The Spatial Landscape of Johannesburg after Apartheid* (Ithaca: Cornell University Press, 2008); Ros Posel, "'Continental Women' and Durban's 'Social Evil,' 1899–1905," *Journal of Natal and Zulu History* 12 (1989): 1–13; Stephen Ramsay, "Eve Noire: 'Folk Devil' and 'Guardian of Virtue': A Study of the Emergence of African Prostitution in Durban at the Turn of the Century," *Journal of Natal and Zulu History* 14 (1992): 75–111; Mariana Valverde, *The Age of Light, Soap, and Water: Moral Reform in English Canada, 1885–1925* (Toronto: McClelland and Stewart, 1991); Judith R. Walkowitz, *City of Dreadful Delight: Narratives of Sexual Danger in Late-Victorian London* (Chicago: University of Chicago Press, 1992).

27. Ash Amin and Nigel Thrift, *Cities: Reimagining the Urban* (Cambridge: Polity, 2002), 95ff; Jennifer Robinson, "Inventions and Interventions: Transforming Cities—An Introduction," *Urban Studies* 43, no. 2 (2006): 252.

28. Ash Amin, "Re-thinking the Urban Social," *City* 11, no. 1 (2007): 103.

29. Ananya Roy and Aihwa Ong: *Worlding Cities: Asian Experiments and the Art of Being Global* (Oxford: Wiley Blackwell, 2011); AbdouMaliq Simone, "On the Worlding of African Cities," *African Studies Review* 44, no. 2 (2001): 15–41.

30. Valverde, *Law's Dream of a Common Knowledge*, 22; Valverde, "Analyzing the Governance of Security," 8; McFarlane, *Learning the City.*

31. David Harvey, "The Political Economy of Public Space," in *The Politics of Public Space*, ed. Setha Low and Neil Smith, 17–34 (New York: Routledge, 2006); Oscar Newman, *Defensible Space. Crime Prevention through Urban Design* (London: MacMillan, 1972); Mariana Valverde, "A Parliament of Uses? A Post-Humanist Approach to Zoning Law and Politics in Urban North America," paper presented at Symposium on Local Spaces, Law and Rights, Bristol University, June 23, 2006; Anthony J. Christopher, *The Atlas of Changing South Africa* (New York: Routledge, 2001).

32. Merry, "Spatial Governmentality and the New Urban Social Order," 16; Richard Warren Perry, "Governmentalities in City-Scapes: Introduction to the Symposium," *Political and Legal Anthropology Review* 23, no. 1 (2000): 65–72; Mariana Valverde, *Diseases of the Will: Alcohol and the Dilemmas of Freedom*

(Cambridge: Cambridge University Press, 1998); Rose and Valverde, "Governed by Law?"; Alan Hunt, "Governing the City: Liberalism and Early Modern Modes of Governance," in *Foucault and Political Reason: Liberalism, Neo-Liberalism and Rationalities of Government*, ed. Andrew Barry, Thomas Osborne, and Nikolas Rose, 167–87 (London: University College London Press, 1996). In Merry's conception, spatial governmentality is both a *concept* that scrutinizes the art of government through spatial means and an emerging *regime* gaining importance globally along with neoliberal approaches to government and an intensification of consumption as identity formation. While not questioning this development toward more complex entanglements of crime control and spatial logics, I would like to use the concept of spatial governmentality as an open toolbox that can contain different, also historic technologies of governing (through) space. This allows us to apprehend the spatial politics of apartheid pass laws with a similar set of questions as, for example, the spatial politics of surveillance cameras in a contemporary city business district.

33. James Holston and Arjun Appadurai, "Cities and Citizenship," in *State/Space: A Reader*, ed. Neil Brenner, Bob Jessop, Martin Jones, and Gordon MacLeod, 296–308 (New York: Wiley-Blackwell, 2003), 297, 301.

34. Nikolas Rose, "Governing Cities, Governing Citizens," in *Democracy, Citizenship, and the Global City*, ed. Engin Fahri Isin, 95–109 (London: Routledge, 2000).

35. James Holston, *Insurgent Citizenship* (Princeton: Princeton University Press, 2007); Engin F. Isin and Greg Marc Nielsen, *Acts of Citizenship* (London: Zed Books, 2008).

36. AbdouMaliq Simone, "The Surfacing of Urban Life," *City* 15, no. 3–4 (2011): 355–64; AbdouMaliq Simone, "Just the City," lecture presented at the Georg Simmel Think and Drink Colloquium, Humboldt University Berlin, May 13, 2013.

37. Shearing and Wood propose the concept of denizen to redefine citizenship, given that "people now live in a world full of criss-crossing memberships that operate across and through multiple and layered governmental domains. . . . The Westphalian world of states monopolising governance, in which political affiliations are understood exclusively in terms of citizenship linked to a social space that extend across states, has been replaced by a multi-layered world of governing auspices. Within this world people operate as denizens of different governmental domains" (Clifford Shearing and Jennifer Wood, "Nodal Governance, Denizenship and Communal Space: Challenges to the Westphalian Ideal" in *Limits to Liberation after Apartheid: Citizenship, Governance and Culture*, ed. Steven Robins [Oxford: James Currey, 2005], 111).

38. Ibid., 105; George S. Rigakos and David R. Greener, "Bubbles of Governance: Private Policing and the Law in Canada," *Canadian Journal of Law and Society* 15, no. 1 (2000): 145–86.

39. Mikhail Bakhtin, "Forms of Time and the Chronotope of the Novel," in Bakhtin, *The Dialogic Imagination*, ed. Michael Holquist, trans. Caryl Emerson and Michael Holquist, 84–258 (Austin: University of Texas Press, 1981). See also Valverde's use of it, for example: Mariana Valverde, *Law and Order: Images, Meanings, Myths* (New Brunswick: Rutgers University Press, 2006).

40. Valverde, *Law and Order*, 138.

41. Doreen B. Massey, *For Space* (London: Sage, 2005), 140.

42. Benoît Dupont, "Mapping Security Networks: From Metaphorical Concept to Empirical Model," in *Fighting Crime Together: The Challenges of Policing and Security Networks*, ed. Jenny Flemming and Jennifer Wood, 35–59 (Sydney: University of New South Wales Press, 2006): 51.

43. Valverde, *Law and Order*, 133.

44. See Jennifer Robinson, "Cities in a World of Cities: The Comparative Gesture," *International Journal of Urban and Regional Research* 35, no. 1 (2011): 1–23.

45. Jamie Peck, "Austerity Urbanism: American Cities under Extreme Economy," *City* 16, no. 6 (2012): 626–55.

46. Valverde, *Law's Dream of a Common Knowledge*; see also Rebecca Pates and Daniel Schmidt, *Die Verwaltung der Prostitution: Eine vergleichende Studie am Beispiel deutscher, polnischer und tschechischer Kommunen* (Bielefeld: Transcript Verlag, 2009), 8–9.

47. Valverde, *Law's Dream of a Common Knowledge*, 22. See also David Garland, *The Culture of Control: Crime and Social Order in Contemporary Society* (Chicago: University of Chicago Press, 2001), 167; David Garland, "'Governmentality' and the Problem of Crime: Foucault, Criminology, Sociology," *Theoretical Criminology* 1, no. 2 (1997): 199; Joyce, *The Rule of Freedom: Liberalism and the Modern City*, 20–21.

48. Interview with Point police officers, 2007; interview with safety and policing adviser, 2006.

49. Valverde, *Law's Dream of Common Knowledge*, 8; Adele Clarke, *Situational Analysis: Grounded Theory after the Postmodern Turn* (Thousand Oaks, Calif.: Sage, 2005), 175.

50. Bruno Latour, *Reassembling the Social: An Introduction to Actor-Network-Theory* (Oxford: Oxford University Press, 2005), 71–72.

51. Ibid., 79.

52. Austin Zeiderman, "Living Dangerously: Biopolitics and Urban Citizenship in Bogotá, Colombia," *American Ethnologist* 40, no. 1 (2013): 71–87.

53. Joe Hermer and Alan Hunt, "Official Graffiti of the Everyday," *Law and Society Review* 30, no. 3 (1996): 456.

54. Thrift, "Movement-Space," 585.

55. Tania Murray Li, *The Will to Improve: Governmentality, Development, and the Practice of Politics* (Durham: Duke University Press, 2007), 9.

56. Valverde, *Law's Dream of a Common Knowledge*, 12.

57. Ibid., 13; Nikolas Rose and Peter Miller, "Political Power beyond the State: Problematics of Government," *British Journal of Sociology* 43, no. 2 (1992): 177.

58. Valverde, *Law's Dream of a Common Knowledge*, 14.

59. Sarah Nuttall, "Literary City," in *Johannesburg: The Elusive Metropolis*, ed. Sarah Nuttall and Achille Mbembe (Durham: Duke University Press, 2008), 191.

60. Achille Mbembe and Sarah Nuttall, "Introduction: Afropolis," in *Johannesburg: The Elusive Metropolis*, ed. Sarah Nuttall and Achille Mbembe (Durham: Duke University Press, 2008), 17.

61. Ibid., 27.

62. Charles Landry, *The Art of City-Making* (London: Earthscan, 2007), 73.

63. Dean, *Governmentality: Power and Rule in Modern*, 268.

64. Ibid., 32.

3. Handsome Space

1. Jonny Steinberg, *Thin Blue: The Unwritten Rules of Policing South Africa* (Johannesburg: Jonathan Ball; Open Society Foundation for South Africa, 2008), 176; see also Clifford Shearing and Julie Berg, "South Africa," in *Plural Policing: A Comparative Perspective*, ed. Trevor Jones and Tim Newburn (London: Routledge, 2006), 208.

2. Patrick Bond, *Elite Transition: From Apartheid to Neoliberalism in South Africa* (Pietermaritzburg: University of KwaZulu-Natal Press, 2005); Tony Roshan Samara, *Cape Town after Apartheid: Crime and Governance in the Divided City* (Minneapolis: University of Minnesota Press, 2011); Martin Murray, *Taming the Disorderly City: The Spatial Landscape of Johannesburg after Apartheid* (Ithaca: Cornell University Press, 2008).

3. Interview with city manager, June 8, 2007, Durban.

4. Most cities today have beautification programs (usually including sidewalk design, street lights, public arts, and flower planting), and they relate these programs to crime prevention. See, for example, Mexico City (http://bigstory.ap.org/article/mexico-city-seeks-beauty-public-space-makeover), Seattle (http://www.seattle.gov/economicDevelopment/biz_district_guide/beautification.htm), Johannesburg (http://www.jhbcityparks.com/index.php/what-we-do-contents-31/major-projects-contents-58/beautifying-our-verges), Baltimore (http://www.promotionandarts.org/arts-council/baltimore-mural-program), Philadelphia (http://www.nbcphiladelphia.com/news/local/Crime-Fighting-Trees-Trans

form-Philly-208895771.html), Cape Town (https://www.capetown.gov.za/en/
MetroPolice2/Pages/Violence-prevention.aspx), and Delhi (http://www.citylab
.com/crime/2014/06/how-urban-design-could-help-reduce-rape-in-india/
372612/). Part of this global move to beautification is the involvement of residents in elements of urban "planning," or "envisioning," as it happened in the
"sensible city" program in Bogota (http://www.miciudadideal.com/en/sensible
_city) or the Warwick Junction initiative in Durban (http://www.designother90
.org/solution/itrump-warwick-junction/).

5. Nigel Thrift, "Intensities of Feeling: Towards a Spatial Politics of Affect,"
Geografiska Annaler 86, no. 1 (2004): 67–68.

6. Ibid., 57.

7. Mariana Valverde, *The Age of Light, Soap, and Water: Moral Reform in
English Canada, 1885–1925* (Toronto: McClelland and Stewart, 1991); Mariana
Valverde, *Diseases of the Will: Alcohol and the Dilemmas of Freedom* (Cambridge:
Cambridge University Press, 1998); Mariana Valverde, *Law and Order: Images,
Meanings, Myths* (New Brunswick: Rutgers University Press, 2006); Alan Hunt,
Governing Morals: A Social History of Moral Regulation (Cambridge: Cambridge
University Press, 1999); Judith R. Walkowitz, *City of Dreadful Delight: Narra-
tives of Sexual Danger in Late-Victorian London* (Chicago: University of Chi-
cago Press, 1992).

8. Ian Loader has made a somewhat parallel argument with regard to
excess in contemporary securitization practices: while excess in the form of
"extravagant violations of law" once informed modern criminological theory
(especially those working with notions of criminals as those who are unable to
"exercise due restraint over their immediate impulses and desires"), today "we,"
as security actors, have come to resemble these criminal types: "impulsive,
short-sighted and increasingly insensitive towards the concerns of those who
'we' define as beyond the ambit of our security priorities, or even as threats to
them." But while Loader suggests understanding public sensibilities and mentalities in terms of an excessive taste for punishment, I am more interested in
seduction and flirtation as a *mode* of governance (Ian Loader, "Ice Cream and
Incarceration: On Appetites for Security and Punishment," *Punishment and
Society* 11, no. 2 [2009]: 245–46).

9. Magistrate of Alexandra, Annual Report on Native Affairs, Alexandra
Division, Natal Archives Repository, 1906, 18.

10. "Darkest Durban: Native 'Public Houses,'" *Natal Mercury*, May 19,
1908; Chief Constable, Addendum to the comparative return of drunkenness
for the borough of Durban, Durban Borough Police, 3/DBN Town Clerns
Office, Kaffir Beer 3, Durban Archives, 1929; Gold Mining & Estate Company,
Report of the Directors and Statement of Accounts, Natal Archives, Pietermaritzburg, December 31, 1898.

11. Report on the Working of the Monopoly System in Durban as provided for under section 21 of the Natives (Urban Areas) Act, 21 of 1923: 5.

12. Paul La Hausse, "Drink and Cultural Innovation in Durban: The Origins of the Beerhall in South Africa, 1902–1916," in *Liquor and Labor in Southern Africa*, ed. J. Crush and C. Ambler (Athens: Ohio University Press, 1992), 99ff.

13. Report on the Working of the Monopoly System in Durban, 4.

14. Paul La Hausse, *Brewers, Beerhalls, and Boycotts: A History of Liquor in South Africa* (Johannesburg: Ravan Press, 1988); David Hemson, "In the Eyes of the Storm: Dock-Workers in Durban," in *The People's City: African Life in Twentieth-Century Durban*, ed. Paul Maylam and Iain Edwards, 67–101 (Pietermaritzburg: University of Natal Press, 1996).

15. The effect of the so-called "Durban System" reached beyond the regulation of African men's beer consumption. The municipality used the revenues earned from the beer monopoly to finance segregated housing for urban African workers and their regimentation through police. See, e.g., Paul Maylam, "Introduction: The Struggle for Space in Twentieth-Century Durban," in *The People's City: African Life in Twentieth-Century Durban*, ed. Paul Maylam and Iain Edwards (Pietermaritzburg: University of Natal Press, 1996), 6; Hemson, "In the Eyes of the Storm," 149. By drinking in the municipal beer halls, African men, as it were, subsidized the police officer who would arrest them under the curfew laws on their way back to the hostel.

16. See Zygmunt Bauman, *Liquid Modernity* (Cambridge: Polity, 2000); Loader, "Ice Cream and Incarceration."

17. Malcolm Feeley and Jonathan Simon, "The New Penology: Notes on the Emerging Strategy of Corrections and Its Implications," *Criminology* 30, no. 4 (1992): 449–74; David Garland, *The Culture of Control: Crime and Social Order in Contemporary Society* (Chicago: University of Chicago Press, 2001).

18. Garland, *The Culture of Control*, 175.

19. Feeley and Simon, "The New Penology," 452.

20. Clifford Shearing, "Governing Security and Making Space," lecture presented at the workshop Governing Security and Making Space, Freie Universität Berlin, September 5, 2008; see further Ronald V. Clarke, introduction to *Situational Crime Prevention: Successful Case Studies*, ed. Ronald V. Clarke, 2–47 (New York: Harrow and Heston, 1997); critically, see Garland, *The Culture of Control*; Lucia Zedner, "Policing before and after the Police: The Historical Antecedents of Contemporary Crime Control," *British Journal of Criminology* 46, no. 1 (2006): 85.

21. Garland, *The Culture of Control*, 171.

22. Oscar Newman, *Defensible Space: Crime Prevention through Urban Design* (London: Macmillan, 1972); James Q. Wilson and George L. Kelling, "Broken Windows," *Atlantic Monthly*, March 1982, 29–37; critically on criminologies of

place see Steve Herbert and Elizabeth Brown, "Conceptions of Space and Crime in the Punitive Neoliberal City," *Antipode* 38, no. 4 (2006): 755–77; Katherine Becket and Steve Herbert, "Dealing with Disorder: Social Control in the Post-Industrial City," *Theoretical Criminology* 12, no. 1 (2008): 5–30.

23. Keith Hayward, "Situational Crime Prevention and Its Discontents: Rational Choice Theory versus the 'Culture of Now,'" *Social Policy and Administration* 41, no. 3 (2007): 235.

24. Bernard E. Harcourt, *Illusion of Order: The False Promise of Broken Windows Policing* (Cambridge, Mass.: Harvard University Press, 2001); Herbert and Brown, "Conceptions of Space and Crime in the Punitive Neoliberal City"; Bernd Belina, *Raum, Überwachung, Kontrolle: Vom Staatlichen Zugriff auf Städtische Bevölkerung* (Münster: Westfälisches Dampfboot, 2006); Gary T. Marx, "What's New about the 'New Surveillance'? Classifying for Change and Continuity," *Surveillance and Society* 1, no. 1 (2002): 9–29; Murray, *Taming the Disorderly City*; Frederick Schauer, *Profiles, Probabilities, and Stereotypes* (Cambridge, Mass.: Harvard University Press, 2003).

25. Gillian Rose, "Performing Space," in *Human Geography Today*, ed. Doreen Massey, John Allen and Phil Sarre (Cambridge: Polity, 1999), 248.

26. Michel de Certeau, *The Practice of Everyday Life* (Berkeley: University of California Press, 1988), 96, 97.

27. Interview with bar owner, April 29, 2008, Durban.

28. Ibid.

29. During later visits to the bar, there were sometimes friendly strong men sitting at the door and checking who went in and out. This is, however, not at the core of the security conception that the bar owner pinpointed. It seems more like a necessary measure that he does not bother mentioning, since employing bouncers and security guards is such a common practice in South African cities.

30. Interview with bar owner.

31. Ibid.

32. Kevin Roberts, "Introduction: The New Consumer: Lovemarks and the Consumer Revolution," in *The Lovemarks Effect: Winning in the Consumer Revolution*, ed. Kevin Roberts, 9–12 (Brooklyn, N.Y.: Powerhouse Books, 2007).

33. See the Lovemarks website at http://www.lovemarks.com.

34. Herbert and Brown, "Conceptions of Space and Crime in the Punitive Neoliberal City."

35. AbdouMaliq Simone, *For the City Yet to Come: Changing African Life in Four Cities* (Durham: Duke University Press, 2009), 12.

36. Point Road was renamed Mahatma Gandhi Road in 2007; the area surrounding the former Point Road is now called South Beach. While the common use is slowly changing to Mahatma Gandhi Road, in the immediate years

after the renaming, "Point Road" and "Point Road area" remained common use, hence I refer to the old names in this chapter.

37. Interview with bar owner.

38. David Lyon, "Introduction," in *Surveillance as Social Sorting: Privacy, Risk, and Digital Discrimination*, ed. David Lyon (London: Routledge, 2003).

39. Martina Löw, *Raumsoziologie* (Frankfurt am Main: Suhrkamp, 2001), 216.

40. Ibid., 204.

41. Thrift, "Intensities of Feeling," 58.

42. Sara Ahmed, *The Promise of Happiness* (Durham: Duke University Press, 2010), 41.

43. Ibid., 26.

44. Durban Point Development Company, "Showcase," Durban, n.d.

45. Durban Point Development Company, "An Investment Opportunity," Durban, n.d.

46. Interview with Point Waterfront security manager, June 8, 2007, Durban; interview with Point Waterfront security manager, April 27, 2008, Durban.

47. Interview with Point Waterfront security manager, June 8, 2007.

48. Point Waterfront, "Daily Report," June 7–8, 2007, Durban: 5.

49. Interview with Point Waterfront security manager, June 8, 2007.

50. Clifford D. Shearing and Phillip C. Stenning, "From the Panopticon to Disney World: The Development of Discipline," in *Situational Crime Prevention: Successful Case Studies*, ed. Ronald V. Clarke (New York: Harrow and Heston Publishers, 1997), 304.

51. Interview with Point Waterfront manager, September 13, 2007, Durban. Similar practices have been reported from other private security companies operating in Durban. Security officers operating at the neighboring beachfront sometimes walk with tourists to help them find their destination, but also to protect them from becoming victims of robbery or assault.

52. Interview with head of Beachfront Unit, Durban Central Police, April 26, 2008, Durban.

53. Interview with Point police officer, March 20, 2006, Durban.

54. On the blending of moral and pragmatic logics of governance see the brilliant work of Valverde, *Diseases of the Will*; Dawn Moore and Mariana Valverde, "Maidens at Risk: 'Date Rape Drugs' and the Formation of Hybrid Risk Knowledges," *Economy and Society* 29, no. 4 (2000), 514–31.

55. Interview with car guard, 4 October 2007, Durban.

56. William J. Novak, *The People's Welfare: Law and Regulation in Nineteenth-Century America* (Durham: University of North Carolina Press, 1996), 70, 14. See also Mariana Valverde, "Analyzing the Governance of Security: Jurisdiction and Scale," *Behemoth: A Journal on Civilisation* 1, no. 1 (2008): 10.

57. Novak, *The People's Welfare*, 52.

58. Ibid., 14.

59. Indeed, bad buildings can be understood as heterotopias, as "counter-sites, a kind of effectively enacted utopia in which the real sites, all the other real sites that can be found within the culture, are simultaneously represented, contested, and inverted." See Michel Foucault, "Of Other Spaces," *Diacritics* (Spring 1986): 24.

60. According to a definition given by the Development Planning Department in the year 2000, the meaning of the term "bad building" is threefold: "In many cases, the buildings, privately owned and publicly owned, are victims of neglect in terms of maintenance by the landlords." These are the derelict or neglected buildings. "In other, more serious situations," the definition continues, "the buildings have become a haven for criminal elements and activities." Finally, "from an economic development point of view, certain buildings in the CBD no longer function properly for current business requirements." But such distinction does not seem to frame the daily assessments of the regulators, both within police and private security and within council (Development and Planning Department, "CBD Revitalization Project: Better Buildings in the CBD," October 2, 2000, Durban).

61. Development and Planning Department, "CBD Revitalization Project."

62. Interview with Better Buildings officer, September 13, 2007, Durban. The Better Building Initiative in Durban is a joint municipal initiative with representatives from City Health, the municipal housing and fire departments, legal services, the inner city's regeneration and management project (iTrump, Metro Police, SAPS), as well as representatives from real estate companies and a community prosecutor. Since the beginning of the project in 2000, the Better Building Initiative has identified a large number of buildings that have been the recipients of interventions, involving a wide range of solutions, from bringing the owners to court, to training body corporates, to sealing off the building or pulling it down.

63. Interview with health manager, May 1, 2007, Durban.

64. Interview with Better Buildings officer.

65. AbdouMaliq Simone, "Pirate Towns: Reworking Social and Symbolic Infrastructures in Johannesburg and Douala," *Urban Studies* 43, no. 2 (2006), 357–70.

66. Interview with Better Buildings officer.

67. Interview with Business Against Crime manager, KZN, June 5, 2007, Durban.

68. Interview with crime prevention officer, Point Police, October 2, 2007, Durban.

69. Interview with iTrump manager, June 6, 2007, Durban; interview with health manager.

70. Interview with Better Buildings officer.

71. Ibid.

72. Interview with Point Waterfront security manager, April 27, 2008.

73. Interview with Point Waterfront security manager, June 8, 2007.

74. For example, a daily report from the security management notes that "CCTV controller saw 1b/m [one black male] behind the Engen garage and S1 [security manager 1] was dispatched to chase him away" (Point Waterfront, "Daily Report").

75. Interview with Point Waterfront manager.

76. Steinberg, *Thin Blue*, 175, 176.

77. See http://durbancto.co.za/general-info/general-information/.

78. See http://www.durbanpeoplemover.co.za (accessed January 20, 2009); for more up-to-date information on the People Mover, see http://www.durban.gov.za/City_Services/ethekwini_transport_authority/Pages/People_Mover.aspx.

79. Ahmed, *The Promise of Happiness*, 39.

80. Interview with strategic projects manager.

81. Interview with iTrump manager, March 13, 2006, Durban.

82. Interview with strategic projects manager.

83. Achille Mbembe, "African Modes of Self-Writing," *Public Culture* 14, no. 1 (2002): 266.

84. Jock Young, *The Exclusive Society* (London: Sage, 1999), 130.

85. Nikolas Rose and Peter Miller, "Political Power beyond the State: Problematics of Government," *British Journal of Sociology* 43, no. 2 (1992): 173–205.

86. Davina Cooper, *Everyday Utopias: The Conceptual Life of Promising Spaces* (Durham: Duke University Press, 2013), 20.

87. Loader, "Ice Cream and Incarceration," 249.

4. Instant Space

1. Zygmunt Bauman, *Liquid Modernity* (Cambridge, Mass.: Polity Press, 2000), 118.

2. Lucia Zedner, "Policing before and after the Police: The Historical Antecedents of Contemporary Crime Control," *British Journal of Criminology* 46, no. 1 (2006): 87. Also see Pat O'Malley and Darren Palmer, "Post-Keynesian Policing," *Economy and Society* 25, no. 2 (1996): 137–55; David Garland, *The Culture of Control: Crime and Social Order in Contemporary Society* (Chicago: University of Chicago Press, 2001); Nikolas Rose and Peter Miller, "Political Power beyond the State: Problematics of Government," *British Journal of Sociology* 43, no. 2 (1992): 173–205.

3. Garland, *The Culture of Control*, 126.

4. David Garland, "The Limits of the Sovereign State: Strategies of Crime Control in Contemporary Society," *British Journal of Criminology* 36, no. 4 (1996): 445–71; Garland, *The Culture of Control*.

5. Ian Loader, "The Anti-Politics of Crime (Review Essay)," *Theoretical Criminology* 12, no. 3 (2008): 401.

6. Mark Shaw, *Crime and Policing in Post-Apartheid South Africa: Transforming under Fire* (Bloomington: Indiana University Press, 2002), 1, 15; William Beinart, "Political and Collective Violence in Southern African Historiography," *Journal of Southern African Studies* 18, no. 3 (1992): 455–86; Michael MacDonald, *Why Race Matters in South Africa* (Cambridge, Mass.: Harvard University Press, 2006); Gary Kynoch, *We Are Fighting the World: A History of the Marashea Gangs in South Africa, 1947–1999* (Athens: Ohio University Press; Pietermaritzburg: University of KwaZulu-Natal Press, 2005).

7. Clive Glaser, "Whistles and Sjamboks: Crime and Policing in Soweto, 1960–1976," *South African Historical Journal* 52 (2005): 119–39.

8. John D. Brewer, *Black and Blue: Policing in South Africa* (Oxford: Clarendon Press, 1994), 200.

9. Clive Glaser, writing on township violence in Soweto in the 1960s and 1970s, points at this very problem of insufficient street lighting (in combination with almost no police presence) and the minimal protection workers had when returning home after dark. Township residents used whistles in order to alert one another of dangers. According to his sources, it was an obligation of "every older person to wake up at whatever time of the night when he hears a whistle" (Glaser, "Whistles and Sjamboks," 134).

10. *Drum* is a popular African magazine that focuses on music, culture, and politics. It was the first transnational popular publication in English circulated in anglophone Africa in both colonial and postcolonial eras, and it became one of the most important media spaces for cultural and political imaginations and debates for black Africans in South Africa and the rest of the continent. The magazine was launched in Cape Town in 1951 as *The African Drum* and owned by Jim Bailey. It later relocated to Johannesburg and, under its new editor Anthony Sampson, rebranded itself as *Drum* and became a symbol of "the new African who, in opposition to apartheid, asserted a city identity." See Michael Chapman, preface to *The Drum Decade: Stories from the 1950s*, ed. Michael Chapman, vii (Pietermaritzburg: University of KwaZulu-Natal Press, 2001); Tom Odhiambo, "Inventing Africa in the Twentieth Century: Cultural Imagination, Politics and Transnationalism in Drum Magazine," *African Studies* 65, no. 2 (2006): 157, 158, 159. The magazine's staff was often harassed by the apartheid government. In fact, the National Party accused *Drum* of being communist and was deeply suspicious of the "bravado of their [urban blacks'] lifestyles, the flamboyance of their dress, or . . . the overeducated English in which they

wrote." See John Matshikiza, introduction to *The Drum Decade: Stories from the 1950s*, ed. Michael Chapman (Pietermaritzburg: University of KwaZulu-Natal Press, 2001), x, xii; Mac Fenwick, "'Tough Guy, eh?': The Gangster-Figure in Drum," *Journal of Southern African Studies* 22, no. 4 (1996): 617, 618.

11. *Drum*, April 1958, 2.

12. Ibid., 17.

13. SA Community Action Network, "Who Are We: Our Passion," http://my-911.com/sacan_new/who-are-we/our-passion.

14. Ash Amin, "Re-thinking the Urban Social," *City* 11, no. 1 (2007): 100–114.

15. Michel Foucault, "Politics and the Study of Discourse," in *The Foucault Effect: Studies in Governmentality: With Two Lectures by and an Interview with Michel Foucault*, ed. Graham Burchell, Collin Gordon, and Peter Miller (Chicago: University of Chicago Press, 1991), 59; Collin Gordon, "Governmental Rationality: An Introduction," in *The Foucault Effect: Studies in Governmentality; With Two Lectures by and an Interview with Michel Foucault*, ed. Graham Burchell, Collin Gordon and Peter Miller (Chicago: University of Chicago Press, 1991), 3; Nikolas Rose, "Government, Authority and Expertise in Advanced Liberalism," *Economy and Society* 22, no. 3 (1993): 289.

16. Nikolas Rose, "Governing Cities, Governing Citizens," in *Democracy, Citizenship, and the Global City*, ed. Engin Fahri Isin (London: Routledge, 2000), 108.

17. Interview with SA CAN duty manager, April 24, 2008, Hillcrest.

18. Interview with SA CAN founder, April 24, 2008, Hillcrest.

19. Ibid.

20. This is an adoption of a line in Khosa writer Isaak Wauchope's poem about the role of intellectuals after the Zulu Rebellion 1906/7. The central idea of the poem was that intellectuals should not fight with a rifle, but with their abilities to think and write, hence, to "fire with your pen" (Wauchape, cited in Albert S. Gérard, *Four African Literatures: Xhosa, Sotho, Zulu, Amharic* [Berkeley: University of California Press, 1971], 41).

21. Rather than implying that there is no police anymore, the phrase is meant to draw attention to a development in which the police force is no longer the only or the most important actor in policing. See also Lucia Zedner, "Policing before and after the Police: The Historical Antecedents of Contemporary Crime Control," *British Journal of Criminology* 46, no. 1 (2006): 81.

22. Interview with EastCoastRadio reporter, September 14, 2007, Durban.

23. *Homo prudens* is the idealized individual who sees crime "as a routine risk to be calculated or an accident to be avoided" (Garland, *The Culture of Control*, 128; see also John Adams, *Risk* [London: University College London Press, 1995], 16). Not only with regard to crime, but in literally every sphere of

their lives, citizens are interpellated as "enterprising selves"—to succeed where society has failed. See Ulrich Bröckling, *Das Unternehmerische Selbst: Soziologie einer Subjektivierungsform* (Frankfurt am Main: Suhrkamp, 2007); Pat O'Malley, "Uncertain Subjects: Risks, Liberalism and Contract," *Economy and Society* 29, no. 4 (2000): 460–84; Nikolas Rose, *Inventing Our Selves: Psychology, Power, and Personhood* (Cambridge: Cambridge University Press, 1996).

24. I spotted this poster in Cape Town, yet I could just as well have discovered it in Durban. I see it as a further illustration of my argument on Durban's responsibilizing and individualizing securisphere. This example from Cape Town points to the fact that my findings, while concentrated on Durban, resonate strongly with developments in urban crime prevention in other South African cities.

25. Interview with EastCoastRadio reporter.

26. Interview with crime mapper, June 7, 2007, Durban.

27. Ibid.

28. Interview with crime mapper, April 29, 2008, Durban.

29. Interview with crime mapper, June 7, 2007.

30. Interview with manager of Department of Community Safety, Province of KwaZulu-Natal, June 4, 2007, Pietermaritzburg.

31. Mariana Valverde, *Law and Order: Images, Meanings, Myths* (New Brunswick: Rutgers University Press, 2006), 133ff.

32. Jean Comaroff and John L. Comaroff, "Figuring Crime: Quantifacts and the Production of the Un/Real," *Public Culture* 18, no. 1 (2006): 230; see also Rose, "Governing Cities, Governing Citizens," 102.

33. See SA Community Action Network, "SA Community Action Network," http://www.sacan.org (accessed September 1, 2008). In recent years SA CAN has merged its different security packages into two single options—one free and one paid: as an "SA CAN member" (without paying fees) one can enjoy access to 24/7 emergency services, while an "SA CAN Family member" (with fees) receives SMS alerts (and MMS alerts with pictures!), panic buttons, a personalized case manager, SOS ID and much more. See SA Community Action Network, "What We Offer: Our Products," http://my-911.com/sacan_new/what-we-offer.

34. Kanishka Goonewardena, "The Urban Sensorium: Space, Ideology and the Aestheticization of Politics," *Antipode* 37, no. 1 (2005): 46–71.

35. SA Community Action Network, "SA Community Action Network," http://www.sacan.org (accessed April 18, 2009).

36. This is different from the usual purposes of "location technologies": surveillance theorist David Lyon outlines that location technologies, such as GPS-enabled cell phones that permit their holders to be tracked as they travel, are often used to control people: employers can check where their employees

are, police may be able to track suspect offenders, and corporations pinpoint the position of consumers in order to send place-specific advertisements. See David Lyon, "The Search for Surveillance Theories," in *Theorizing Surveillance: The Panopticon and Beyond*, ed. David Lyon (Cullompton, U.K.: Willan Publishing, 2006), 115.

37. Rose, "Governing Cities, Governing Citizens," 100. Don Mitchell offers a related imaginary of a floating bubble around a person entering a health clinic that provides abortions. This bubble cannot be pierced—i.e., violated—by anti-abortion protesters. Mitchell sees such a protective bubble as a kind of moving privacy in public space, resulting from the United States Supreme Court decisions about a "right to be left alone" in public. See Don Mitchell, "The S.U.V. Model of Citizenship: Floating Bubbles, Buffer Zones, and the Rise of the 'Purely Atomic' Individual," *Political Geography* 24 (2005): 87.

38. See SA Community Action Network, "SA Community Action Network," http://www.sacan.org/ (accessed September 1, 2008).

39. Interview with SA CAN duty manager.

40. A striking aspect in the seat belt metaphor as brought forward by the SA CAN manager is the idea of *everybody* wearing a seat belt: It underlines the *pars pro toto* conception of *everyone* discussed above. The SA CAN duty manager certainly means *almost everybody*, and almost everybody *who is in a car*, wears a seat belt. These generalizations make sense in the social context in which they are being stated. *Everybodies* are those in cars; they are not the ones walking down the street.

41. Interview with EastCoastRadio reporter.

42. The incidence of crime is seen as comparable to the incidence of an accident. Writing on risk and accidents, John Adams describes how accidents are seen as "the result of a mistake, a miscalculation, a lapse of concentration, or simple ignorance of the facts about a dangerous situation." Discussions on minimizing risks for accidents are "inhabited by Homo prudens—zero-risk man. He personifies prudence, rationality and responsibility. . . . Homo prudens strives constantly, if not always efficaciously, to avoid accidents. Whenever he has an accident, it is a mistake' or 'error.' When this happens, if he survives, he is acutely embarrassed and he tries, with the help of his expert advisers, to learn from his mistakes." See Adams, *Risk*, 16.

43. Reader's Digest Association South Africa, *Safe, Secure, and Streetwise: The Essential Guide to Protecting Yourself, Your Home, and Your Family from Crime*, (Cape Town, 1997), 8.

44. See SA Community Action Network, SA CAN Family Matters, e-mail newsletter, November 17, 2009.

45. Reader's Digest Association South Africa, *Safe, Secure, and Streetwise*.

46. Strategic Projects Unit, *We Are Durban: Durban Information Guide* (Durban, 2009), 15.

47. Reader's Digest Association South Africa, *Safe, Secure, and Streetwise*, 130.

48. Zygmunt Bauman, *Consuming Life* (Cambridge, Mass.: Polity Press, 2007), 52, 55.

49. Bauman, *Consuming Life,* 54.

50. Bauman, *Liquid Modernity,* 76–77.

51. Ian Loader, "Ice Cream and Incarceration: On Appetites for Security and Punishment," *Punishment and Society* 11, no. 2 (2009): 252.

52. Interview with SA CAN duty manager.

53. Ibid.

54. Ibid.

55. SA Community Action Network, SA CAN Family Matters, e-mail newsletter, October 18, 2009.

56. Interview with SA CAN duty manager.

57. SA Community Action Network, *Change Is Coming: Business Plan* (2008), 6.

58. Judith Butler, *Frames of War: When Is Life Grievable?* (London: Verso, 2009), 31.

59. Interview with organized crime commissioner, Special Task Team, KwaZulu-Natal, September 13, 2007, Durban.

60. Ibid.

61. There is a fund within the South African Police Service that allows (and encourages) police officers to recruit informers who might provide them with information about crime. Depending on the value of the information, the informer can be remunerated with a considerable amount of money. However, none of the car guards that I met have ever received money for sharing information with the police.

62. Interview with car guard, October 4, 2007, Durban.

63. Interview with car guard, April 26, 2008, Durban.

64. Ibid.

65. The typical negative assumption about car guards' criminal involvement goes like this: "Sometimes you have car guards that are working with perpetrators as well. . . . Because certain syndicates want a Toyota Corolla that's white in color, a Toyota Corolla will be stolen. Now syndicates would have to . . . drive around, try to locate a white Toyota Corolla. Why doesn't he just pick up his phone and phone all his car guards: 'Do you have a white Corolla there?' . . . Knowing that he is operating under the protection to an extent of the car guard, who stands in that area every night, who has been monitoring the white Corolla every night parking till four in the morning every night, who knows

that the police is generally not patrolling at two in the morning, because they are having a snooze, so he gives his perpetrator the information. 'I've got a white Toyota Corolla here. Come and take it at about two o clock, because there is no much policemen'" (interview with safety and policing adviser, March 14, 2006, Durban).

66. Lieven De Cauter, "The Capsule and the Network: Notes toward a General Theory," in *The Cybercities Reader*, ed. Stephen Graham (London: Routledge, 2004), 96.

67. Rowland G. Atkinson, "The Flowing Enclave and the Misanthropy of Networked Affluence," in *Networked Urbanism: Social Capital in the City*, ed. Talja Blokland and Mike Savage (London: Ashgate, 2008), 42, 47.

68. AbdouMaliq Simone, *For the City Yet to Come: Changing African Life in Four Cities* (Durham: Duke University Press, 2004); AbdouMaliq Simone, "People as Infrastructure: Intersecting Fragments in Johannesburg," *Public Culture* 16, no. 3 (2004): 407–29; Achille Mbembe, "Democracy and the Ethics of Mutuality," lecture presented at the Johannesburg Workshop in Theory and Criticism, Wits University, Johannesburg, July 6, 2009.

69. Simone, "People as Infrastructure," 408.

CONCLUSION

1. AbdouMaliq Simone, "Taking the City by Surprise—Part One," *blog villes noires*, December 3, 2013, http://villes-noires.tumblr.com/post/68929339970/taking-the-city-by-surprise-part-one.

2. On a critique of John and Jean Comaroff's *Theory from the South: or, How Euro-America Is Evolving toward Africa* (Boulder, Colo.: Paradigm Publishers, 2012) along those lines see James Ferguson, "Theory from the Comaroffs, or How to Know the World Up, Down, Backwards and Forwards," *Johannesburg Salon* no. 5 (2013): http://jwtc.org.za/salon_volume_5/james_ferguson.htm.

3. Jennifer Robinson, *Ordinary Cities: Between Modernity and Development* (London: Routledge, 2006); Ananya Roy, "The 21st-Century Metropolis: New Geographies of Theory," *Regional Studies* 43, no. 6 (2009): 819–30; Comaroff and Comaroff, *Theory from the South*; Swati Chattopadhyay, *Unlearning the City: Infrastructure in a New Optical Field* (Minneapolis: University of Minnesota Press, 2012).

4. Aihwa Ong, "Introduction: Worlding Cities, or the Art of Being Global," in *Worlding Cities: Asian Experiments and the Art of Being Global*, ed. Ananya Roy and Aihwa Ong, 1–26 (Oxford: Wiley Blackwell, 2011); Achille Mbembe and Sarah Nuttall, "Writing the World from an African Metropolis," *Public Culture* 16, no. 3 (2004): 347–72.

5. Raewyn Connell, *Southern Theory: The Global Dynamics of Knowledge in Social Science* (Cambridge, Mass.: Polity Press, 2007).

6. Ackbar Abbas, "Poor Theory and New Chinese Cinema: Jia Zhangke's 'Still Life,'" lecture presented at the Critical Theory Institute, University of California, Irvine, December 3, 2008, 14.

7. Edgar Pieterse, "Grasping the Unknowable: Coming to Grips with African Urbanisms," *Social Dynamics* 37, no. 1 (2011): 5–23; Mbembe and Nuttall, "Writing the World from an African Metropolis," 353.

8. James Holston, *Insurgent Citizenship* (Princeton: Princeton University Press, 2007); James Holston and Teresa Caldeira, "Urban Peripheries and the Invention of Citizenship," *Harvard Design Magazine* (Spring/Summer 2008): 17–23; Engin F. Isin and Greg M. Nilesen, *Acts of Citizenship* (London: Zed Books, 2008).

9. Valverde has argued with reference to Scott that "seeing like a city" is not "seeing like a small state" but qualitatively different. See Mariana Valverde, "Analyzing the Governance of Security: Jurisdiction and Scale," *Behemoth: A Journal on Civilization*, no. 1 (2008): 5.

10. Colin McFarlane: *Learning the City: Knowledge and Translocal Assemblage* (Malden, Mass.: Wiley-Blackwell, 2011).

11. Sherry Turkle, *The Second Self: Computers and the Human Spirit* (Cambridge, Mass.: MIT Press, 2005), 13.

12. McFarlane, "Learning the City," 3.

13. Ann Laura Stoler, "Imperial Debris: Reflections on Ruins and Ruination," *Cultural Anthropology* 23, no. 2 (2008): 191–219; Achille Mbembe, "Aesthetics of Superfluity," *Public Culture* 16, no. 3 (2004): 373–405.

14. AbdouMaliq Simone, "Just the City," lecture presented at the Georg Simmel Think and Drink Colloquium, Humboldt University Berlin, May 13, 2013.

15. "Flirt, v.," *OED Online* (Oxford: Oxford University Press), OED.com.

16. Ash Amin, *Land of Strangers* (Cambridge, Mass.: Polity Press, 2012), 10.

17. Achille Mbembe, "Democracy as a Community of Life," *Johannesburg Salon*, no. 4 (2013): 2.

18. Hillary Angelo and Craig Calhoun, "Beneath the Social: Invitation to an Infrastructural Sociology," unpublished article (2013).

19. AbdouMaliq Simone, "Infrastructure: Introductory Commentary by AbdouMaliq Simone," Curated Collections, *Cultural Anthropology Online* (November 26, 2012), http://www.culanth.org/curated_collections/11-infrastructure/.

20. Angelo and Calhoun, "Beneath the Social."

21. Mbembe, "Democracy as a Community of Life."

Index

affect, 4, 58; spatial politics of, 2, 13, 54, 58, 61, 113, 118, 123
affective calculus, 58
affective power of spaces, 2, 12, 13, 31, 39, 54, 57, 58, 62–64, 70, 86, 113
Ahmed, Sara, 69–70, 81, 87
apartheid nostalgia, 21
apartheid spatiality, 31, 39; and Bantustans, 28, 33–34; and compartmentalization, 32–34; and Graphism, 33; and group areas act, 31–32; and homeland, 28–29, 32–33; and segregation, 37, 45. *See also* space; spatial governance
atmosphere, 49, 54, 69; colors, 49–50, 62, 65; decoration, 2, 65–66, 119; music, 2, 10, 62, 65, 66, 73, 119; power of, 58, 66; sensual cues, 64. *See also* affect; beauty; handsome space

bad buildings, 64, 74–76, 78
Bantustans, 28, 33–34
beautification, 57–58
beauty, 58, 61, 74, 79, 87; and aesthetics, 4, 13, 53, 63, 106; power

of, 58, 74, 79. *See also* atmosphere; beautification; handsome space
beer halls, 35, 59, 60, 62
broken windows policing, 4, 13, 58, 61–62, 86. *See also* criminologies of place
bubble: of governance, 2, 46–47, 62, 70; handsome, 63, 85; of imagined safety, 13, 37, 114, 121; instant, 113; mobile, 3, 81; relationship between city and, 62–63, 78, 87

Cato Manor, 32
chronotope, 2, 46, 47, 62, 70, 72, 74, 82, 86
City Improvement Districts, 2, 30, 38, 44, 78, 122
cityness, 4, 7, 113, 115, 120
class apartheid, 39; inequality and, 5, 29, 31, 69, 78, 118; new segregation and, 31, 38–39
Comaroff, John and Jean, 9, 16–17, 19, 24, 25, 102
crime mapping, 49–50, 89, 99, 101–2
criminologies of place, 5, 62, 66, 91, 92, 106, 112

Dean, Mitchell, 53
de Certeau, Michel, 63
defensible space, 4, 61, 113. *See also*
    criminologies of place
denizen, 11, 46, 59, 64, 70, 72, 74, 86,
    119, 121, 125
Durban: Cato Manor in, 32; char-
    acter of, 7–9; demographics of, 8;
    suburb of Hillcrest and, 96, 108;
    World Cup 2010 in, 7, 16, 50, 54,
    105. *See also* beer halls; Durban
    People Mover; Point Road area;
    Point Waterfront
Durban People Mover, 63, 79, 81–82,
    85, 87
Drum magazine, 26, 92–95

epistemic wallpaper, 11, 13, 42, 48,
    51–53

Feeley, Malcolm M., 60, 61
fleeing, 54, 55; as logic of self-
    governance in instant space, 2,
    118–21. *See also* navigation
flirting, 2, 54–55; as logic of gover-
    nance in handsome space, 118–20,
    122; mingling with moralizing
    techniques, 62; promise of security
    and, 66, 79, 87; and seduction, 39,
    44, 58, 60, 66, 106. *See also* affect;
    handsome space
Foucault, Michel, 5, 7, 34, 42, 52
fragmentation, 1, 2, 5, 12, 13, 14, 31,
    37, 39, 69, 97, 113; texture of, 57;
    and new segregation, 31, 38–39

Garland, David, 60, 91
governance, 1–3, 6, 8–10, 13–14, 16,
    29–30, 34, 39–49, 52–55, 57–59,
    61–63, 70–71, 74, 86, 91–92, 97,
    99, 103–4, 109, 113–14, 119;

through space, 54, 86, 118, 121;
    urban, 1, 6, 8, 39, 41, 48, 57
governmentality, 7, 10, 11, 45, 52, 86,
    91; and government (Foucault), 7,
    11–12, 42; and self-government, 7,
    96; spatial, 45. *See also* state: of
    South Africa
Graphism, 33

handsome space: atmosphere of, 49,
    54, 69; as attribute for regime of
    spatial security governance, 2,
    13–15, 30, 36, 40, 54–55, 58–66,
    68–69, 74, 76, 78, 79, 82, 85–87,
    91, 99, 107, 113, 118, 121–23; charm
    initiatives and, 57; flirting and, 2,
    54–55; seduction and, 39, 44, 58,
    60, 66, 106. *See also* beauty;
    happiness
happiness: of a place, 70, 87; and
    well-being of a place, 64. *See also*
    handsome space; welfare

infrastructure: people as, 114; beneath
    the social, 123
instant space, 2, 13–15, 19, 30, 36,
    40, 54, 55, 89, 91, 92, 95–99, 102–
    7, 110, 113–15, 121–23; avoiding
    crime and, 91, 92, 95, 98; here-
    and-now matters and, 5, 47,
    76, 85–86, 91–92, 119, 122; the
    power of fleeing, 2–3. *See also*
    navigation

Latour, Bruno, 50
Loader, Ian, 87, 106
lovemarks: and capitalism, 69, 123;
    in city branding, 66
low-status expert knowledge, 13, 42,
    48–51
Lyon, David, 36

Mbembe, Achille, 3, 6, 7, 20, 21, 25, 26, 32, 33, 34, 35, 39, 53, 123

navigation: through insecurity, 14, 54, 89, 97; outsmarting crime through, 91, 117; as responsibilization, 11, 27, 28, 30, 91, 99, 114; and structural failure, 95; and survival, 7, 11, 14, 15, 26, 30, 45, 98, 113, 115, 120, 121, 122. *See also* instant space
necropolitics, 3, 4, 34–35. *See also* Mbembe, Achille
new culture of control, 5, 60–61. *See also* Garland, David
new penology, 60–61. *See also* Feeley, Malcolm M.; Simon, Jonathan
nonhuman actants, 2, 47, 49, 50, 64, 65, 66
Nuttall, Sarah, 3, 6, 16, 36, 53

People Mover. *See* Durban People Mover
Pieterse, Edgar, 7
plural policing, 12, 28, 43; and private security companies, 10, 25, 29, 44, 49, 51, 62, 73, 79; and security patchworking, 30
Point Road area (Durban), 8, 64, 67, 72, 81
Point Waterfront (Durban), 64, 70–73, 78–83
postapartheid: crime politics, 4, 12, 20, 21, 23, 24, 29, 95, 117, 121, 122; politics of space; 1–2, 13, 30–31, 36, 38, 39–40, 54, 55, 57, 62, 76, 85, 114; state, 8, 16, 21, 30
postcolonializing urban research, 6–7; and comparative urbanism, 9
postcolony, 8, 19, 117

private security companies, 10, 25, 29, 44, 49, 51, 62, 73, 79

regime of practices, 53
responsibilization, 11, 27, 28, 30, 91, 99, 114
Robinson, Jennifer, 6
Rose, Gillian, 12, 63

salus bubbli, 74
salus populi, 73, 74, 78
Samara, Tony, 16
SAP (South African Police), 21, 28, 29
SAPS (South African Police Service), 17, 21, 28
security: as continuous striving, 113; governance of, 9, 46; as ideal, 41, 92, 97, 107, 112, 114; and insurance-like arrangements, 103; as pursuit, 11, 12, 42, 47, 87; and securisphere, 10, 47, 48, 51; as self-care, 95; spatial life of, 14, 41, 62, 121; as situational experience, 3, 91, 113
seeing like a city, 13, 42, 44, 45, 46, 47, 48, 55. *See also* Valverde, Mariana
Shearing, Clifford, 29, 46, 71; and Jennifer Wood, 46
shebeens, 26, 59–60. *See also* beer halls
Simon, Jonathan, 60, 61
Simone, AbdouMaliq, 7, 114, 117
situational crime prevention, 4–5, 62, 86. *See also* criminologies of place
social sorting: in apartheid South Africa, 35–36, 69; in postapartheid South Africa, 13, 39, 114. *See also* spatial governance
South African Police. *See* SAP

South African Police Service. *See* SAPS

space: doing, as technique of security, 12, 63, 99; governing through, 54, 86, 118, 121. *See also* apartheid spatiality; postapartheid: politics of space

spatial governance: apartheid spatial governance, 1, 34; postapartheid spatial governance, 2, 30, 40, 45, 54. *See also* apartheid spatiality; social sorting

state: accountability, 21, 28; social contract, 21; of South Africa, 19–20, 21, 23, 24, 28–29, 31, 50

statistics: black on black crime, 23; as discursive currency, 19; and political priorities, 23; and profiling, 17, 19, 25, 47; sanitation, 17; of township violence, apartheid, 12

surface: cosmetic fallacy of, 5, 85; as new root cause of crime, 5, 66, 74, 76, 86; and obsession of postapartheid spatial transformation, 5, 64, 85–86; and underneath, 5, 7, 53

survival, 7, 11, 14, 15, 26, 30, 45, 115, 120, 121; math, 98, 113

survivalzenship, 121–22

survive-style, 97, 99, 104–7, 115

Thrift, Nigel, 51, 58

urban citizen: as citizen of the bubble, 14, 55, 89, 97–99, 101, 103, 104, 107, 108–10, 111–13, 114, 122; as homo prudens, 11; responsibilized, 11. *See also* denizen; survivalzenship

Urban Improvement Precincts, 10, 62

Valverde, Mariana, 13, 42, 46, 48, 52

Waterfront. *See* Point Waterfront

welfare: people's, 73–74; of a place, 73; salus bubbli, 74; salus populi, 73, 74, 78

(continued from page ii)

VOLUME 17
Mobile Urbanism: Cities and Policymaking in the Global Age
EUGENE MCCANN AND KEVIN WARD, EDITORS

VOLUME 16
Seeking Spatial Justice
EDWARD W. SOJA

VOLUME 15
Shanghai Rising: State Power and Local Transformations in a Global Megacity
XIANGMING CHEN, EDITOR

VOLUME 14
A World of Gangs: Armed Young Men and Gangsta Culture
JOHN M. HAGEDORN

VOLUME 13
El Paso: Local Frontiers at a Global Crossroads
VICTOR M. ORTÍZ-GONZÁLEZ

VOLUME 12
Remaking New York: Primitive Globalization and the Politics of Urban Community
WILLIAM SITES

VOLUME 11
A Political Space: Reading the Global through Clayoquot Sound
WARREN MAGNUSSON AND KARENA SHAW, EDITORS

VOLUME 10
City Requiem, Calcutta: Gender and the Politics of Poverty
ANANYA ROY

VOLUME 9
Landscapes of Urban Memory: The Sacred and the Civic in India's High-Tech City
SMRITI SRINIVAS

VOLUME 8
Fin de Millénaire Budapest: Metamorphoses of Urban Life
JUDIT BODNÁR

VOLUME 7
Latino Metropolis
VICTOR M. VALLE AND RODOLFO D. TORRES

VOLUME 6
Regions That Work: How Cities and Suburbs Can Grow Together
MANUEL PASTOR JR., PETER DREIER, J. EUGENE GRIGSBY III,
    AND MARTA LÓPEZ-GARZA

VOLUME 5
*Selling the Lower East Side: Culture, Real Estate, and Resistance in
    New York City*
CHRISTOPHER MELE

VOLUME 4
*Power and City Governance: Comparative Perspectives on Urban
    Development*
ALAN DIGAETANO AND JOHN S. KLEMANSKI

VOLUME 3
Second Tier Cities: Rapid Growth beyond the Metropolis
ANN R. MARKUSEN, YONG-SOOK LEE, AND SEAN DIGIOVANNA,
    EDITORS

VOLUME 2
Reconstructing Chinatown: Ethnic Enclave, Global Change
JAN LIN

VOLUME I
The Work of Cities
SUSAN E. CLARKE AND GARY L. GAILE

CHRISTINE HENTSCHEL is assistant professor of international criminology at Hamburg University.